Presidential Leadership and the Creation of the American Era

THE RICHARD ULLMAN LECTURES

COSPONSORED WITH THE WOODROW WILSON SCHOOL OF
PUBLIC AND INTERNATIONAL AFFAIRS, PRINCETON UNIVERSITY

*Presidential Leadership and the
Creation of the American Era*
by Joseph S. Nye, Jr.

Presidential Leadership and the Creation of the American Era

JOSEPH S. NYE, JR.

PRINCETON UNIVERSITY PRESS
PRINCETON, NEW JERSEY

Library of Congress Cataloging-in-Publication Data
Nye, Joseph S.
Presidential leadership and the creation of the
American era / by Joseph S. Nye, Jr.
pages   cm. — (Richard Ullman Lectures)
Includes bibliographical references and index.
ISBN 978-0-691-15836-5 (hardcover : alk. paper)
1. Presidents–United States. 2. Political leadership—
United States. 3. Executive power—United States.
4. United States—Politics and government. I. Title.
JK516.N94 2013
352.23'60973—dc23   2012051152

British Library Cataloging-in-Publication Data is available

TO MOLLY

★

Our detached and distant situation invites and enables us to pursue a different course. . . . Why forego the advantages of so peculiar a situation? Why quit our own to stand upon foreign ground?
　—*George Washington, Farewell Address, 1796*

My dream is that as the years go by and the world knows more and more of America it . . . will turn to America for those moral inspirations which lie at the basis of all freedom. . . . All shall know that she puts human rights above all other rights and that her flag is the flag not only of America, but of humanity.
　　　　—*Woodrow Wilson, 1917*

Throughout the 17th century and the 18th century and the 19th century, this continent teemed with manifold projects and magnificent purposes. Above them all and weaving them all together into the most exciting flag of all the world and of all history was the triumphal purpose of freedom. . . . It is in this spirit that all of us are called, each to his own measure of capacity, and each in the widest horizon of his vision, to create the first great American Century.
　　　　　—*Henry Luce, 1941*

CONTENTS

Preface

xi

CHAPTER 1

The Role of Leadership

1

CHAPTER 2

The Creation of the American Era from
Theodore Roosevelt to George H. W. Bush

21

CHAPTER 3

Ethics and Good Foreign Policy Leadership

75

CHAPTER 4

Twenty-First-Century Leadership

136

Notes

161

Index

175

Americans are fascinated by their presidents. And they like America's primacy in world politics. In the 2012 presidential campaign, both candidates vowed that American power was not in decline and they would maintain American primacy. But how much are such promises within the power of presidents to keep? Were presidents essential to the establishment of American primacy, or was it an accident of history that would have occurred no matter what type of leader occupied the Oval Office?

For more than two decades, I have been studying the sources and nature of American power, and speculating about its future. I have been skeptical of the conventional cycles of belief in American decline that sweep public and elite opinion every decade or so, including the current one that started after the 2008 financial crisis. But my arguments have rested on larger structural forces in the United States and in the world, rather than on the role of the individuals who led the country. In this book I turn to the question of whether presidents mattered in the creation of American primacy, and what the answer tells us about their role in the future of American power. International relations experts often refer to three "images" of reality—the system of states, the state, and the individual. They all too rarely look seriously at the role of individuals. In the pages that follow, I try to reconcile international relations and individual leadership theory.

Leadership experts extol the virtues of transformational leaders who set out bold objectives to change the world, and analysts tend to downplay the role of transactional leaders with more modest objectives as mere managers. Contrary to that conventional wisdom, I conclude below that some presidents matter, but not always the ones who are most dramatic or inspiring. Over the past century in which the United States assumed primacy in world politics, some presidents tried with varying degrees of success to forge a new international order while others sought mainly to manage America's existing position. But looking at the eight leaders who presided over the key periods of expansion of American primacy, I found to my surprise that while transformational presidents like Woodrow Wilson and Ronald Reagan changed how Americans see the world, transactional presidents like Dwight Eisenhower and George H. W. Bush were sometimes more effective and more ethical. I would not have come to this unconventional conclusion before I undertook this study.

This book suggests that President Obama and his successors should beware of thinking that transformational proclamations are the key to successful adaptation to the rapidly changing politics of a global information age. American power and leadership will remain crucial for stability and prosperity at home and abroad, but honing their contextual intelligence and remembering their transactional predecessors' observance of the Hippocratic oath ("above all, do no harm") will provide future presidents better guidance than stirring calls for transformational leadership.

This book grew out of a course I taught at Harvard's Kennedy School of Government for a number of years. I am grateful to many students for sharp questions that made me rethink my answers. I am also grateful for the support of the Center for Public Leadership under the able leadership of David Gergen. I have also gained great intellectual support from my colleagues at the Belfer Center for Science and International Affairs. Its director, Graham Allison, not only read carefully but provided insights during fly-fishing excursions that ranged from the Adirondacks to Alaska.

A number of colleagues and friends read portions of the manuscript and contributed ideas. Although he never had a chance to read the final manuscript, Ernest May read an early draft of chapter 2 and provided his thoughts in many conversations. Bob and Nan Keohane read through many drafts and provided multiple ideas while we hiked in the mountains of Maine and New Hampshire. Other friends who read and commented included Robert Blackwill, Michael Doyle, Fred Greenstein, Barbara Kellerman, Andrew Moravcsik, Gautam Mukunda, Robert Rotberg, Anne-Marie Slaughter, Kenneth Winston, Ali Wynne, and Philip Zelikow. Chuck Myers of Princeton University Press not only commissioned the book but provided sage advice through several drafts. I was honored to be chosen to deliver the basic ideas in lectures in honor of Richard Ullman, a friend since Oxford, Harvard, and the 1980s Project at the Council on Foreign Relations. Jessica Brandt was an excellent research assistant, and Jeanne Marasca provided invaluable general assistance. So many people have provided important ideas and general help over the years that I cannot begin to list them all, but I am fortunate to have such supportive friends. Above all, I am grateful for the support of Molly Harding Nye, who has been my leader for more than half a century, and to whom this book is dedicated.

Joseph Nye
Sandwich, NH

Presidential Leadership and the Creation of the American Era

CHAPTER 1

The Role of Leadership

At the end of the twentieth century, the United States was the world's sole superpower. References to American empire or hegemony exaggerate the extent to which America could control the rest of the world, and I prefer the term "primacy" to describe the way in which, by the end of the century, the United States became the only country with global military, economic, and cultural reach. Contrary to theory and modern history, American power went unbalanced. As one expert observed, "It is highly unusual for a country with only 5 percent of the world's population to be able to organize favorable political, economic and security orders in almost every corner of the globe and to sustain them for decades."[1]

It was not always thus. In the early days of the republic, George Washington noted America's "detached and distant situation" and asked "why forego the advantages of so peculiar a situation?" It proved to be an interesting question that Americans have wrestled with throughout their history, and most recently over the course of the twentieth century. How did American primacy come about?

Social scientists tend to answer with structural theories that are attractive because they appear to provide broad general explanations. Everything seems inevitable. We humans are embedded in complex structures of culture, social relations, and power that affect and constrain us. In a perfect market, for example, a wheat farmer has no pricing power. Millions of other unseen farmers and consumers making independent choices create the market supply and demand that determines the price. Structure overwhelms agency. Different analysts cut into the complex pattern of causation and draw the line between individual choice and larger structures at different places, but as Karl Marx correctly observed, people do not make history under conditions of their own choosing.

In international structural theories, liberals have stressed technological changes in transport and communication that increased global interdependence and made America's situation behind two oceans less distant from the rest of the world. Marxists emphasize the global imperatives of capital, trade, and profit. Realists note the growth of American power resources and argue that expansion of powerful states is almost a law of nature. As Henry Kissinger has argued, "No nation has ever experienced such an increase in its power without seeking to translate it into global influence."[2] But what role did human agency play? Scholars of international relations refer to different levels of explanation and tend to discount the level that relies on individual choices.[3]

In contrast, leadership theorists place a heavy emphasis on individuals and their relations with various circles of followers. Can we reconcile these approaches? How important was presidential leadership in shaping the American era? Did the United States have good foreign policy leadership in the twentieth century, and how much did it matter in creating the situation of unprecedented primacy that runs against the predictions of balance of power theory? Did presidents matter? If we took out the leadership variable, would America still have come to exercise primacy in international politics?

Even in the nineteenth century, the United States could not avoid some entanglement with Europe, but the 1823 Monroe Doctrine, which reserved our interests in the Western Hemisphere, depended on British, not American, sea power. Moreover, the United States used its military and economic power within the hemisphere to expand to the Pacific at the expense of Mexico and Native American peoples. What has been called "isolationism" looked quite different from the perspective of Mexico City. American exceptionalism meant moralism about European power politics, not necessarily morality. But by and large, the United States remained largely isolated from the global balance of power. In the late nineteenth century, "the national government treated foreign relations much like it did the rest of its business. In almost all cases the initiative lay elsewhere. . . . Foreign relations were composed of incidents, not policies."[4]

Behind its oceans, however, the American economy continued to grow, as did its role in global trade and finance. In 1880 Great Britain represented 23 percent of world industrial production and the United States 15 percent. By 1900 America was at 23 percent and Britain at 19 percent.[5] The United States became the world's largest economy by the beginning of the twentieth century, accounting for nearly a

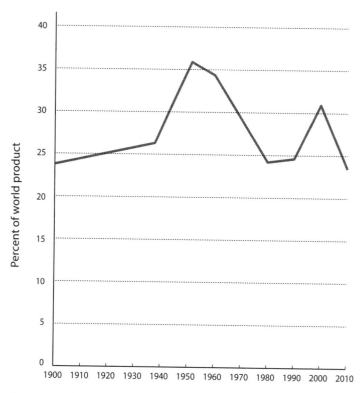

Figure 1. The United States share of world GDP. This figure is based on three authorities: (1) Herbert Block's estimate that in the early twentieth-century the United States accounted for almost a quarter of world product; (2) Simon Kuznets's estimate that the United States represented 29.5 percent of world income in 1938; and (3) the World Bank's World Development Indicators, which cover the period from 1960 to present.

quarter of world product. By 1918 American intervention proved decisive to the outcome of World War I. After World War II America produced nearly half the world's product and had an atomic monopoly, but those advantages eroded over the next quarter century. Some saw this as decline, but it might be better described as the recovery of the others. At the end of the century, the United States represented about the same share of world product as at the beginning, but its political role was incomparably greater.

From a structural point of view, American primacy might seem inevitable as American power resources increased, but there are anomalies for simple structural explanations. Even during the period of its greatest domination in share of power resources after World War II, the United States was unable to obtain its preferences on a number of important issues,[6] and the return to its normal share does not explain the changes in the last quarter of the century. Why were there long periods when the United States shirked an international role? And why did the American order take the shape of what some analysts have termed "liberal hegemony" rather than a more imperial form?[7]

What role did individual leadership play? One of the problems of leadership theory is "leader attribution error."[8] Something goes right or wrong and we attribute the result to the leader. Losing sports teams fire their coaches, and profitable companies give raises to their CEOs. But conjunction in time does not prove causation or establish the strength of an effect. To what extent were the men who presided over the creation of the American era simply responding, or were they shaping events? Sometimes leaders not only take a fork in the historical road but help to create it. Such leaders are often called transformational in the sense of changing what would otherwise be the course of history. They raise new issues and new questions. "Good politicians win the argument. Every now and then someone comes along and changes it."[9] For example, after September 11, 2001, any American president might have responded with force to the Taliban government's provision of sanctuary to Al Qaeda in Afghanistan, but in choosing to also invade Iraq, George W. Bush created a fork in the road and became, for better or worse, a transformational leader.

Leaders have different degrees of effect on history, and change is often a matter of degree. Political leaders matter "a little more, a little less, depending on how they diagnose those problem situations for their political communities, what responses they prescribe for meeting them, and how well they mobilize the political community's support for their decisions."[10] We know that in some conditions leaders matter more than in others, particularly in fluid times of crisis, and getting the details of causation right provides work for generations of historians. Since each age has access to new facts, incorporates new biases, and raises new questions, even careful judgments change over time. Theodore Roosevelt was a popular president who brought American foreign policy into the twentieth century. In contrast, Woodrow Wilson's foreign policy of promoting democracy and the League of Nations was a failure by the end of his term and was rejected by the American people for two decades after his presidency. Nonetheless, Henry Kissinger argues that, by the middle of the century, Wilson's ideas had more influence on American opinion than did Teddy Roosevelt's.[11]

What do we compare and when do we judge? History does not produce final verdicts because each age reinterprets the past in the light of its own interests and preoccupations. Nonetheless it seems useful to distinguish leadership in advancing ideas from leadership in implementing policy actions, and to set temporal thresholds such as the end of an administration or a decade as preliminary judgment points. By these criteria, for example, Wilson may have been a leader in codifying certain ideas that had deep roots in both European and American liberal tradition, but he clearly failed as a transformational policy leader in his own time. Successful transformation requires both vision and implementation.

TRANSFORMATIONAL LEADERSHIP

For the past three decades, writers about leadership have placed a great deal of emphasis on transformational leaders and the term is widely used, though in confusing ways. According to James McGregor Burns, who developed the term in 1978, transformational leaders use conflict and crisis to raise their followers' consciousness and transform them by appealing to their "higher ideals and moral values rather than baser emotions of fear, greed, and hatred."[12] Followers are thus inspired to undertake adaptive work and respond to change for the good of the group. Transactional leaders, on the other hand, rely on the hard power resources of carrots and sticks to appeal to their followers' self-interest. One source of confusion, however, is that Burns builds values into his definition. Thus a Hitler, who clearly transformed Germany for the worse, cannot be a transformational leader by definition. In general it is better to distinguish questions of good or bad from questions of effectiveness, so in this book the ethical questions will be dealt with in a separate chapter.

A second reason leadership theorists and editorial writers are often confusing is that they use the term "transformational" to refer to leaders' objectives, the styles leaders use, and the outcomes they produce. Those three dimensions of what a leader seeks, what methods he or she uses, and what he or she achieves are not the same thing. Sometimes a leader may transform the world and not transform his followers, or vice versa, and sometimes she may use a transactional style to accomplish transformational objectives.[13]

Franklin Roosevelt is often cited as an example of a transformational leader, and in the 1930s he used the soft power of inspirational vision and communications to help achieve his transformational goals of social reform, transforming the views of his followers in the process. American government and politics were never again the same. But in foreign policy Roosevelt was unable to transform American isolationist attitudes, and he used very indirect *transactional* bargaining methods to pursue his goal of moving American foreign policy toward support of Great Britain before World War II. His followers were ready for transformation on social issues but not on foreign policy, so he adopted transactional methods. Harry Truman is another example of a successful leader who developed transformational objectives while in office but tended to be transactional in his style. And sometimes a leader who seeks primarily incremental changes, like Bill Clinton, will use inspirational methods.

Given this confusion in the theory, I will use different terms to describe leaders' objectives and their styles. Leaders' objectives can range on a scale from status quo through incremental to major change. I will call those who

TABLE 1.1. LEADERS' OBJECTIVES AND STYLES

	Transactional style	Inspirational style
Transformational objectives	Harry Truman	Woodrow Wilson
Status quo/incremental objectives	Dwight Eisenhower	Bill Clinton

seek major change *transformational leaders* and those at the other end of the scale *incremental leaders*. We can distinguish leaders' styles by how they use hard and soft power resources. I will use the term *transactional style* to characterize the skills with which leaders manage their hard power resources for coercion and payment, and *inspirational style* to characterize leadership that rests more on soft power skills of attraction and persuasion. Thus the opposite of a transactional style is inspirational, not transformational. Sometimes people call such a style charismatic, but that term is so fraught with ambiguity and confusion that it is better to avoid it.[14] Table 1.1 illustrates how one can have transformational leaders who mostly use a transactional style (Truman); transformational leaders who are strong on inspirational style (Wilson); incremental leaders with a transactional style (Eisenhower); and incremental leaders who often use an inspirational style (Clinton).

Of course leaders do not fit neatly in boxes, and all try to adopt different styles in different contexts.[15] Franklin Roosevelt did not enter office with a clear game plan for the American economy, and he experimented with a variety of domestic changes. Clinton tried to pass an ambitious health-care bill and also to strengthen the United Nations, but he curtailed his objectives after early defeats. Similarly, as we

will see in chapter 4, Barack Obama proclaimed transformational foreign policy goals in his 2008 campaign but followed mainly incremental policies in his first term in office.
Change is a matter of degree, and many leaders seek it on
some issues and not others. Nonetheless leaders generally
tend toward a predominant style. By definition, transformational leaders seek major change, and their objectives can
be scaled in terms of the degree and scope of change they
seek.[16] Whether they succeed in achieving their ambitious
objectives is a third question. If not, they are "would-be" or
"failed" transformational leaders. A leader can be transformational in intentions but not in outcomes.

Leaders may also deliberately change their objectives
and style over the course of their career. For example, one
of the great transformational leaders in the history of international politics, Otto von Bismarck, was transformational
in his goals before he achieved the unification of Germany
under Prussian leadership, but largely incremental and status quo–oriented after that success. And as we shall see
below, Franklin Roosevelt changed his foreign policy objectives and style quite dramatically during his presidency.
His objectives were incremental in his first term but became
transformational in the second half of his second term.

Scholars argue that transactional leadership styles are
more effective in stable and predictable environments, and
an inspirational style is more likely in periods of rapid
and discontinuous social and political change. The transformational objectives and inspirational style of a leader
like Mohandas Gandhi or Nelson Mandela can make all
the difference to outcomes in fluid social situations, particularly in developing countries where there are weakly

structured institutional constraints.[17] In contrast, the context of American foreign policy formation is highly constrained by institutions like Congress, courts, and the Constitution. Thus we would expect less opportunity for transformational leadership. But even the US Constitution is ambiguous about the powers of the president and Congress in foreign policy. At best it creates what the great constitutional scholar Edward S. Corwin called "an invitation to struggle."[18] Also, much depends on external conditions. Teddy Roosevelt entered office with transformational objectives in foreign policy, but Wilson, Franklin Roosevelt, and Truman developed such objectives only in response to external events after they entered office.

Crisis conditions can liberate a gifted leader from the accumulated constraints of vested interest groups and bureaucratic inertia that normally inhibit action in the American system. Bill Clinton, caught up in the complacent 1990s, is said to have envied Franklin Roosevelt's crisis conditions of the 1930s.[19] Potential followers experience new or accentuated needs and look for new guidance. Action becomes more fluid. For instance, George W. Bush used the crisis conditions after September 11, 2001, to make strong assertions of the executive power of the presidency as well as to invade Iraq. When followers feel the need for change, a leader with transformational objectives faces better odds, and an inspirational style is more likely to find responsive followers and to make their role more relevant. Turbulent times may set the scene for transformational leaders, but it does not follow that bold and risk-loving leaders are always best suited to deal with the crises that define turbulent times.[20]

SKILLS OF AN EFFECTIVE LEADER

Whether they are transformational or incremental in their objectives, leaders need certain soft and hard power skills to be effective, and these too are a matter of degree. The presence or absence of these skills affects the methods and styles that leaders use. Among the soft power skills are emotional intelligence (emotional self-control and the ability to use emotional cues to attract others); vision (an attractive picture of the future that balances ideals, objectives, and capabilities); and communication (the ability to use words and symbols to persuade both an inner circle and a broader audience). With regard to the use of hard power resources, two hard power skills are particularly important: organizational capacity and the Machiavellian political skills of bullying, buying, and bargaining in the formation of winning coalitions.

Above all, effective leadership requires the skill of contextual intelligence, an intuitive diagnostic skill that helps a leader understand change, interpret the outside world, set objectives, and align strategies and tactics with objectives to create smart policies in new situations. As Singapore's Lee Kuan Yew once put it, a leader must be a quick learner, testing reality and being prepared to change his mind as conditions change, and then act calmly in a crisis.[21] Contextual intelligence implies both a capability to discern trends in the face of complexity as well as adaptability while trying to shape events. Bismarck once referred to this skill as the ability to intuit God's movements in history and seize the hem of his garment as he sweeps by.[22] More prosaically, like surfers, leaders with contextual intelligence

TABLE 1.2. EFFECTIVE LEADERSHIP:
SOFT AND HARD POWER SKILLS

Soft power (inspirational)	
Emotional IQ	Able to manage relationships and apply personal charisma
	Has emotional self-awareness and control
Communication	Persuasive to followers by words, symbols, example
Vision	Attractive and effective (balances ideals and capabilities)
Hard power (transactional)	
Organizational capacity	Uses reward and information systems for inner and outer circles
Machiavellian skills	Able to bully, buy, bargain, and build winning coalitions
Smart power (combined resources)	
Contextual IQ	Understands evolving environment
	Capitalizes on trends ("creates luck")
	Adjusts style to context and followers' needs

have the ability to judge and adjust to new waves and then ride them to success.

Contextual intelligence allows leaders to adjust their style to the situation and to their followers' needs. It enables them to create flows of information that "educate their hunches." It involves the broad political skill of not only sizing up group politics, but understanding the positions and strengths of various stakeholders so as to decide when and how to use transactional and inspirational skills. It is the self-made part of luck. In unstructured situations, it is often more difficult to ask the right questions than to get the right answer. Leaders with contextual intelligence are skilled at providing meaning or a road map by defining the problem that a group confronts. They understand the tension between the different values involved in an issue, and how to balance the desirable with what is feasible. In particular, contextual intelligence requires an understanding of groups' cultures, the distribution of power resources, followers' needs and demands, information flows, and timing.[23]

Presidential Leadership in Creating American Primacy

How important was good presidential leadership in explaining the major steps in the creation of the American era? The word "good" is ambiguous because it can mean ethical or effective or both, and the two aspects do not always coincide. In chapter 2 I will ask how effective were the leaders who presided over the creation of the American era, and whether leaders with strong transformational objectives were more effective than more incremental leaders. In chapter 3 I will turn to the question of how ethical the two types of leaders were. Chapter 4 will summarize my conclusions about the role of presidents in the creation of American primacy in the twentieth century as well as discuss the implications for presidential foreign policy leadership in the twenty-first century.

What twentieth-century presidents should we look at? Not all contributed to the creation of American primacy.

TABLE 1.3. PHASES IN THE DEVELOPMENT OF
TWENTIETH-CENTURY AMERICAN PRIMACY

1. Entry into the global balance of power: T. Roosevelt, Taft, Wilson

2. Return to normalcy and isolation: Harding, Coolidge, Hoover

3. Entry into World War II: F. Roosevelt

4. Containment and permanent presence abroad: Truman, Eisenhower

5. Vietnam and overextension: Kennedy, Johnson

6. Post-Vietnam adjustment: Nixon, Ford, Carter

7. End of the Cold War and unipolarity: Reagan, G.H.W. Bush, Clinton

Rather than looking solely at transformational presidents (which would have the disadvantage of what social scientists call selecting on the dependent variable), I will look at the eight presidents who were in office during the four major stages of the expansion of American primacy. Dividing a century into phases is always somewhat arbitrary, but from the point of view of development of American primacy, at a first approximation one can identify seven major phases, four of which involved major increases in America's role and power in the world, and three of which were marked by relative stasis or even a diminution of America's role.

Four of these phases contributed to primacy; and three led to contraction or stasis. I am interested in the four positive periods. For the first expansionist phase, America's entry into the global balance of power, I will compare how Theodore Roosevelt, William Howard Taft, and Woodrow

Wilson responded to the rise of American power resources and their failed transformational efforts to create a new order. For the second expansionist phase, America's entry into World War II, I will examine Franklin Roosevelt's response to the rise of German and Japanese power and his efforts to escape isolationism. The third expansionist stage was Harry Truman's successful transformation of Roosevelt's grand strategy into a permanent presence of American troops overseas at the beginning of the Cold War. I will then look at the role of Dwight Eisenhower, who is generally considered an incremental and transactional leader but played a crucial role in consolidating the new international order of containment. For the fourth phase of the creation of the American era, I will compare the role of Ronald Reagan, a transformational leader, with that of George H. W. Bush, a mostly incremental leader with a transactional style, in ending the Cold War and establishing the unipolar world in which American primacy reached its peak with the collapse of the Soviet Union in December 1991.

This principle of selection and comparison allows me to test the impact of transformational leadership on the creation of the American era, but it is important to be clear that this book is not an examination of all transformational leaders, nor all the important events in twentieth-century American foreign policy. For example, during the 1920s the Harding administration negotiated the Washington naval arms control agreements and the Coolidge and Hoover administrations launched the Dawes and Young plans for dealing with European financial problems. None, however, was willing to fill the security vacuum that became chronic as American attitudes hardened into full-fledged isolationism in the 1930s.

Similarly, I do not examine the 1960s and 1970s, though they included John F. Kennedy's deft handling of the Cuban Missile Crisis, Richard Nixon's important opening to China, and Jimmy Carter's raising of the priority of human rights and nuclear nonproliferation, because I am not trying to present a complete history of leadership in twentieth-century American foreign policy. There is no detailed discussion of the leaders who presided during the punctuation periods of interwar isolationism or Vietnam or the post-Vietnam adjustment. Again, my focus is not on transformational leadership in twentieth-century foreign policy. Rather, I am asking the question of whether good leadership (and what types) contributed to the creation of the unprecedented American primacy that developed in the previous century.

Some readers may object to my treatment of the Vietnam and post-Vietnam period, but it reflects my judgment that the Vietnam War was a period that set back rather than advanced the creation of twentieth-century American primacy. It is true that Kennedy's rhetoric about vigor and some of his policies advanced American power, but his regime was cut too short to have a major effect on the creation of American primacy, and his debatable legacy in Vietnam was greatly expanded by Lyndon Johnson and wound up setting America back. By weakening the army, unleashing inflation, destroying foreign policy consensus at home, and straining relations with allies and other countries, the

Vietnam War diminished American hard and soft power in the world.[24] While the Vietnam War may have bought some time for countries like Singapore and Indonesia to develop autonomously, American primacy would have advanced more rapidly without the Vietnam War. This irony was well illustrated in 2012 when the Vietnamese government invited the American defense secretary to visit the former American military base in Cam Rahn Bay as part of diplomatic balancing of China's rising power. If American leaders had framed the East Asian balance as a nationalist game of checkers rather than an ideological game of dominoes, they could have reached a better outcome at much lower levels of cost.

Richard Nixon inherited this Vietnam legacy and wisely created an opening to China as a means of changing the focus of attention away from the impasse.[25] His opening to China was transformational and one of the important steps of twentieth-century American foreign policy. But it was an adjustment to a diminished reality rather than a step in the creation of American primacy. As Robert W. Tucker wrote, "The logic of the Nixon reformulation, with its centerpiece of détente, was the logic of retrenchment."[26] Nixon (and Henry Kissinger) believed that the United States was losing power. Détente, the opening to China, and the Nixon doctrine of relying on regional powers such as Iran were adjustments to what Nixon saw as the crumbling of bipolarity as the Soviets gained strategic nuclear equivalence and China developed a second-strike capability. He and Kissinger accepted the view that the correlation of forces was moving in the Soviets' favor. As late as 1979 Kissinger predicted that because of American nuclear weakness, Soviet risk taking would exponentially increase.[27] Neither Kissinger nor Nixon foresaw that within two decades the Soviet economy would collapse and bipolarity would be replaced by unipolarity rather than their expected multipolarity. While Nixon's opening to China may have contributed somewhat to the pressures on the Soviet Union, it was not the major source of the stress that brought down the Soviet Union (as will be discussed below).

Nixon was also concerned about the importance of economic change and tried to respond in a transformational way. In his words, "It's terribly important we be number one economically because otherwise we can't be number one diplomatically or militarily."[28] As we saw in figure 1, the American share of world product had been artificially expanded by the way that World War II had weakened other major economies while strengthening that of the United States. By the late 1960s the American share had returned to its normal one quarter of world product that it held before both world wars.

Nixon realized that the artificial American dominance of the world economy that had been created by World War II was gradually eroding, and he was concerned about a balance-of-payments crisis unless he raised the price of gold or took domestic steps to control inflation at the cost of unemployment and domestic political risk. Instead he chose the third option of ending the convertibility of the dollar into gold, imposed illegal temporary tariffs, and shifted the costs of adjustment onto allies without any international consultation. Breaking the Bretton Woods international economic system that the United States had helped create in 1944 fit Nixon's desire to make dramatic gestures (he called it "showmanship"),[29] but he had no vision and little interest in the future of the monetary system, paid little attention to economic details, and excluded his secretary of state and national security advisor from the decision process that ended the Bretton Woods system. Tactically Nixon was successful for a brief period, but over the longer term he left Gerald Ford and Jimmy Carter with a legacy of uncontrolled inflation and worsened relations with allies that contributed to a weakening of American power in the 1970s. As one careful study concluded, the foresight "that came naturally to him in respect of his strategic decision making about China and Russia did not appear in his thinking about economic policy, save with respect to the electoral imperative of November 1972. Instead he allowed himself to be beguiled by the prospect of quick political reward from quack economic remedies."[30] Nixon's international economic actions of 1971 did not contribute to the expansion of American primacy.

In the next two chapters, I will look at the eight leaders who presided over the four positive phases of the expansion of American power in terms of their effectiveness and ethics. Finally, in the fourth chapter, I will ask what lessons we can learn about good foreign policy leadership in a twenty-first century where the American order confronts a new environment with major power shifts from West to East, and from states to nonstate actors.

The Creation of the American Era from Theodore Roosevelt to George H. W. Bush

Leadership is a process of interaction among leaders, followers, and the context in which they act. As we have seen, the context of America's role in the world began to change in the late nineteenth century. The American economy surpassed Britain's in manufacturing in 1885, though the United States was perceived at home and abroad as a weak player in global politics with an army of only twenty-five thousand and a navy smaller than that of Chile. While President Grover Cleveland was prepared to face down Britain over a border dispute between Guyana and Venezuela in 1895, his action was consistent with the traditional Monroe Doctrine of hemispheric exclusion. However, some elites were beginning to think of a more global American role, notably Alfred Mahan with his views on sea power in history, which influenced Theodore Roosevelt and others.[1]

A large but temporary change in America's role in the world occurred in 1898 when the United States started the Spanish-American War and entered a brief period of taking colonies, the most striking departure being the seizure of Spain's Philippine Islands colony in the distant Pacific.

As recently as 1871 the United States had turned down
an invitation of annexation from the Dominican Republic,
and in the 1880s the young Theodore Roosevelt echoed
most educated public opinion in opposing colonization.[2]
But in the 1890s, as Ernest May has shown, American elite
attitudes split under the influence of social Darwinism, the
psychological closing of the frontier, and the influence of
European imperial ideas and example. Briefly there was a
consensus for possessing overseas colonies (which Roosevelt actively abetted in his role as undersecretary of the
navy). President William McKinley agreed to the annexa-
tions, but he was not leading the charge, merely reacting to
his followers. McKinley was an incremental not a transformational leader. By 1900 the brief episode was over, with
public opinion turning unfavorable to further colonization
in reaction to the Philippine insurrection, liberal opposition to the Boer War, and the anti-imperialist candidacy of
William Jennings Bryan in that year's presidential election.
The first excursion of the United States into global politics
did not last long and was not the result of presidential leadership. America's brief flirtation with overseas colonialism
turned out to be neither a true transformation nor guided
by the top leader.

The First Phase: America Enters the Global Balance of Power

America's real entry into global politics occurred in the
twentieth century under three presidents—Theodore Roosevelt, Taft, and Wilson—though as we shall see Taft was
primarily an incremental leader. (Historians generally rank

Roosevelt and Wilson in the top quartile of American presidents and Taft in the second or third quartile.) The transformational leaders were Roosevelt and Wilson. Both were later to win a Nobel Prize for their actions while in office; Ivy League graduates; authors of books; strong believers in America's special god-given mission in the world; and inspirational in style and transformational in their progressive domestic agendas. But there the similarities end. The two leaders disliked each other and saw the world in very different ways.

With greater experience and interest, Roosevelt had better contextual intelligence about global affairs and was able to perceive the gradual changes that were favoring American interests well before his followers and the American public did. Wilson, on the other hand, came into office focused on domestic policy and acted outside the Western Hemisphere only when the crisis of World War I was totally apparent (if not similarly interpreted) by his followers and a majority of the public. While Roosevelt's contextual intelligence helped him to perceive change and formulate a transformational foreign policy objective before he became president, Wilson entered office with incremental foreign policy goals. He developed transformational goals only in the context of the crisis created by Germany's resumption of unrestricted submarine warfare after he was reelected in 1916.

Theodore Roosevelt

Teddy Roosevelt was the first president to deliberately project American power on the global stage. While he had an important idealist strand of thought growing out of his faith in American exceptionalism and the

civilizing mission of the Anglo-Saxon peoples, his operational worldview was that of a realist who saw the shifting
global balance of power. His famous speech about walking
softly and carrying a big stick came in the first year of his
presidency (1901), but such early actions as management
of the 1902–3 Venezuela Crisis and the ensuing Roosevelt
Corollary to the Monroe Doctrine and intervention in the
Dominican Republic were traditional rather than transformational. His interest in building the navy, pressing
Britain to revise the Clayton-Bulwer Treaty that restricted
American construction of an isthmus canal, and abetting
Panama's secession from Colombia had extrahemispheric
as well as regional implications. But many of these and
other successes in asserting American power, such as set-
tling the Alaskan boundary and Newfoundland fisheries
disputes on American terms, might have occurred under
any president—even his incremental successor, William
Howard Taft.

Roosevelt's real innovation was in his perception of the
shifting balance of power in Europe and Asia, and the steps
he took to insert the United States into it. While he could
be tough with Britain when it came to hemispheric issues,
for cultural and geopolitical reasons he saw a congruence
of interests and sought an alignment of policies. He mistrusted the rising powers of Russia and Germany but was
cautiously encouraging to the rise of Japan in Asia. His
mediation of the Russo-Japanese War resulted in the Treaty
of Portsmouth in 1905, which recognized Japan's new role
but did not overly weaken Russia in the Asian balance. As
one historian noted, "The United States could not make

war in East Asia, so Roosevelt made peace. It was, under the circumstances, a brilliant maneuver."[3]

Roosevelt's role as a "man of peace" was popular at home (and won him a Nobel Peace Prize abroad) but was not seen by the American public as a shrewd maneuver of inserting America into the global balance of power. As for his involvement a year later in helping to mediate the first Moroccan Crisis between Germany and France, the public was largely unaware, and Roosevelt largely kept Congress out of it. The Taft-Katsura conversation in 1905 and the Root-Takahira agreement of 1908, in which the United States acquiesced in allowing Japan a free hand in Korea in return for forbearance in the Philippines, were also given little public attention. On the other hand, defeating the Philippine insurrection and promising preparation for ultimate independence were very public, as of course was the decision to send the Great White Fleet on a round-the-world cruise from December 1907 to February 1909. That journey helped send a message to Japan about American power in Asia, but at home it was interpreted mainly as a symbol of American pride.

Roosevelt did little to educate the American public about his strategic vision. As a result, he succeeded in transforming the way the United States was perceived and acted globally as a power, but not in transforming the way in which the American public saw their role in the world. Roosevelt's leadership transformed America's role in the world but not his followers' views, and thus his impact was limited. Not only did he fail to educate the public, but he had a disdainful view of the slow-moving Congress, an essential part of the American foreign policy process. William Tilchin argues that "TR did his best to educate without undermining his various diplomatic endeavors,"[4] but it was not enough. Henry Kissinger exaggerates when he writes that Roosevelt's "approach to international affairs died with him in 1919; no significant school of American thought on foreign policy has invoked him since."[5] Franklin Roosevelt was influenced by his older cousin as well as by Woodrow Wilson, and the design for a United Nations that improved on the League of Nations shows the influence of Teddy Roosevelt's realism. Other elements of his vision that included belief in American exceptionalism and a civilizing mission also persisted. But if transformational leadership involved profoundly changing the views of one's followers about America's role in the world, Teddy Roosevelt was a failed transformational leader, as evidenced by his discontent with his successors' policies. Ironically, for the man who extolled the presidency as a "bully" pulpit and used it to transform domestic affairs, he was unable to use it to transform the public understanding of American foreign policy. In that sense, despite the most engaging and energetic of styles, and a number of significant accomplishments, Roosevelt mainly failed as a transformational leader in foreign policy.

William Howard Taft

Taft was Roosevelt's friend, loyal supporter, and chosen successor, but Roosevelt and other progressive Republicans became disillusioned with what they saw as Taft's undue conservatism. Roosevelt's decision to run as a third-party candidate in the 1912 election split the Republican vote and deprived Taft of a second term. As Elihu Root observed about Roosevelt, "when he gets into a fight, he is completely dominated by the desire to destroy his adversary completely."[6] Taft was personally devastated by Roosevelt's action. He had served effectively under Roosevelt as governor-general of the Philippines and secretary of war. Indeed, his judicious temperament and popularity among many Filipinos had helped Roosevelt to overcome that difficult episode.

Taft came from a prominent Republican family in Ohio, and his father had served as secretary of war and attorney general under Ulysses Grant. After graduating from Yale and Cincinnati Law School, he practiced law and served on the Ohio Superior Court. In 1890, when Taft was thirty-two, President Benjamin Harrison appointed him solicitor general of the United States, and two years later he was confirmed for the federal court of appeals. Taft was a very large man who used his size effectively on the wrestling team at Yale, but his temperament was sometimes described as phlegmatic at worst or judicious at best.

Taft's inclination was toward the law rather than politics. He lacked his predecessor's charisma and inspirational communication skills, and as president he failed to cultivate the press as Roosevelt did. He often made statements and took decisions that seemed to disdain partisan politics, though his success in obtaining and implementing administrative appointments, and later in working with Congress, showed that he possessed some transactional political skills. Taft's greatest aspiration, however, was to be on the

Supreme Court, and he was eventually appointed chief justice by President Warren Harding in 1921. Ironically, Taft had turned down earlier opportunities to be appointed to the Supreme Court out of deference to his executive branch duties under Roosevelt. Had he joined the court instead, Wilson would not likely have been elected and (as we shall see below) history might have been different.

Taft considered himself a moderate progressive, and his domestic policy followed largely in the direction set by Roosevelt, but the Republican Party was split between progressive and conservative wings, and Taft lacked Roosevelt's political skills to manage them. Despite the latter's complaints of inadequate zeal, Taft launched more antitrust suits than Roosevelt, lowered tariffs despite the opposition of many industries, and saw the Sixteenth Amendment, establishing an income tax, passed during his presidency. Overall Taft's attitude was more probusiness and less environment friendly, and he lacked Roosevelt's expansive view of the powers of the executive branch. The big difference, however, was on foreign policy.

Roosevelt once mistakenly believed that "if Taft succeeds me our foreign policy will go on absolutely unchanged."[7] But this is an example where types of leadership made a major difference. Taft did not have deeply different views on foreign policy from Roosevelt's. "Taft represented a new breed of American statesmen who had become acutely conscious of America's expanding power in the world." Moreover, "not even Theodore Roosevelt could boast of such broad foreign experiences upon becoming president."[8] A few years later, by means of more than fifty speeches and articles supporting the League of Nations, Taft proclaimed the end of isolation and said that "were Washington living today, he would not consider the League as an entangling alliance."[9]

But Taft's leadership skills were completely different from Roosevelt's. By rising to power through the judiciary and appointed roles, "Taft was never forced to develop the knowledge and skills of the professional politician concerned with winning and maintaining public support. He was neither a stirring orator, a flatterer of the people, nor a sensitive barometer of the passing whims and fancies of the populace. . . . Surprisingly, he could admit to his wife in the midst of the 1906 congressional campaign, 'Politics, when I am in it, makes me sick.' "[10] And it did not help his position that he followed one of the most skilled and popular politicians, who continued to meddle in power.

Taft appointed Philander Knox, a corporate attorney with little experience in foreign affairs, as his secretary of state. Knox would often come to the office at ten in the morning and leave after lunch, but Taft was a strict believer in delegation, and he eschewed the personal role that Roosevelt played in foreign policy. "Taft actually insulated himself from the flow of information essential to his own political success by becoming overly dependent upon official lines of communication." Moreover, he failed to inspire "that camaraderie and loyalty to the chief executive which had marked the Roosevelt administration."[11] In the Machiavellian and organizational political skills listed in table 1.2, Taft was a total contrast to his predecessor.

Taft's foreign policy was sometimes dubbed "dollar diplomacy." As he said in a 1912 speech, "the diplomacy of the present administration has sought to respond to modern ideas of commercial intercourse. This policy has been characterized as substituting dollars for bullets."[12] Where Roosevelt was the hunter and warrior who disdained business, "under Taft, the business of American diplomacy was business."[13] He encouraged loans for railway building and tried to advocate the open door policy in China, but without great success. Taft's major concerns were the traditional worry about stability in the Western Hemisphere and the new interest of protecting the Panama Canal. By having the State Department encourage loans by American banks to the region, he would restrict European interests and interventions. This was reinforced by American interventions such as seizing the customs houses in Nicaragua and Haiti. At the same time, he was cautious about intervening in the early stages of the Mexican Revolution. As for a global role, Taft's legalistic approach sought to promote world peace through law, and he negotiated treaties of arbitration with Britain and France. Amendments in the Senate watered down his willingness to accept limits on sovereignty in such treaties. "The agreements marked a potentially radical departure from the traditional nationalism of American diplomacy and were so interpreted by the Senate."[14] Moreover, a bold trade reciprocity agreement with Canada failed in that country's legislature.

While American economic strength continued to grow throughout the Progressive Era, Taft did little to build on it to increase the American role in world politics. He preserved Roosevelt's legacy in the Western Hemisphere and tried to keep an open door in China, but he did little to add to his predecessor's efforts to chart a global role. Taft was clearly incremental rather than transformational in his objectives, and transactional rather than inspirational in his style of presidential leadership. He contributed little to the creation of primacy.

Woodrow Wilson

Like Teddy Roosevelt, Woodrow Wilson was a transformational leader in establishing the progressive reform movement in domestic policy, but he was initially little interested in foreign policy. His early interventions in Mexico and the Caribbean were reactive, rather naïve, and very much in the American foreign policy tradition. Yet Wilson presided over a pivotal point in America's involvement in global politics when he sent two million troops to fight in a European war. This was an enormous departure from tradition, and even from Teddy Roosevelt's approach. Roosevelt saw World War I partly in terms of Anglo-American civilization, but also in balance-of-power terms. He was clear that American interests were aligned with Britain's, and he lobbied for American entry on Britain's side early in the war. The question is whether he would have been able to bring the American people along with him at that early stage. Public opinion was deeply divided, and Wilson won the 1916 election by promising to keep the country out of the war.

Wilson disliked the concept of power balances. He referred to "the great game, forever discredited, of the balance of power."[15] He felt that there should be a more principled approach to global order that would be more consistent with American moral principles. At one point, after German U-boats sank the *Lusitania* in 1915, he proclaimed that "there is such a thing as a man being too proud to fight . . . and a nation being so right that it does not need to convince others by force that it is right."[16] During his first term he insisted on neutrality and sent his aide Colonel House to Europe to try to mediate a peace without victors. Wilson expressed his objective in very incremental terms up until the beginning of 1917. All that while, Teddy Roosevelt was criticizing Wilson for his moralistic approach and his failure to understand the importance of force and to see the American interests in an Allied victory.

Shortly after winning reelection in November 1916, however, Wilson was confronted by Germany's resumption of unrestricted submarine warfare (as well as the provocative Zimmerman telegram trying to stir up trouble in Mexico). Feeling trapped, Wilson largely relied on his own counsel in early 1917. He looked carefully at three major options: continued neutrality; armed neutrality to try to protect ships at sea; and full entry into the war on the side of the Allies.[17] Rather than pursuing the cautious middle option, Wilson chose the most audacious (as Roosevelt urged), but he then did something Roosevelt would not have done. While Roosevelt might have explained the balance-of-power reasons for entry into the war, Wilson wrapped his choice in American moralism. In presenting his fourteen points to Congress and the world, he outlined a new set of principles including a league of nations for a more moral order in world politics that would be consistent with what he saw as American values.

Wilson was not an original thinker in foreign affairs. His "essential contribution to this ferment was propagation and grand synthesis. . . . Nothing less than a new international political ideology."[18] While he had communicated with Lord Grey about a league in 1916, and the ideas were inherited in part from British liberalism, it was in the context of the crisis of February 1917 that Wilson formulated his transformational objectives. He prevailed in persuading a majority of the American people to follow him, and in the successful prosecution of the war at home and in Europe. This entry into the war was transformational in both objective and outcome, and it is not clear that another president (such as Roosevelt) could have been as successful. In the short run Wilson transformed the views of his followers to support an action totally at odds with the existing American foreign policy tradition. But he had two transformational objectives: to change American foreign policy and to change the very nature of world politics, and he linked the two together.

Wilson was an early proponent of public diplomacy to promote American soft power. He established a Committee on Public Information under the journalist George Creel, which became a highly effective propaganda machine with global reach. "For Wilson, spreading the American gospel and winning world opinion to the side of U.S. ideas was a crucial war aim. The American mission to transform international relations, he thought, could succeed only if others were convinced that a transformation was necessary and desirable: 'everything that affects the opinion of the world regarding us,' the president told his secretary of state, 'affects our influence for the good.'"[19]

Where Wilson failed, of course, was in transforming the attitudes of other world leaders, and ultimately the American public, about the new world order he had outlined.

Initially European crowds treated him as a hero, but as the haggling in Versailles dragged on for six months, the nationalist constituents of Clemenceau, Lloyd George, and Orlando proved more deeply rooted and persistent.[20] At Versailles Wilson compromised on many of his fourteen points in order to obtain agreement on the Covenant of the League of Nations, with its obligations of collective security in which countries pledged to ally against any aggressor rather than to balance other powers. But on return to the United States, he refused to compromise with Senator Henry Cabot Lodge, even instructing Democratic supporters to vote against the treaty rather than compromise. Wilson thought his inspirational style would win over the public, but his barnstorming speaking tour in the autumn of 1919 was cut short by illness.

By the time of the final negotiations, when Wilson stubbornly refused to compromise and the Senate killed the treaty, he was a very sick man. Ironically if the stroke he suffered in 1919 had killed rather than debilitated him, the Senate would probably have ratified the treaty, and the United States would have joined the new League of Nations. Whether American participation could have staved off the events in Manchuria and Ethiopia that contributed to the demise of Wilson's collective security in the early 1930s is uncertain, but in the meantime the compromises he made at Versailles to obtain the League undercut his other great principle of self-determination by establishing situations like German minorities in Czechoslovakia and in the Danzig Corridor in Poland that proved to be political time bombs Hitler would detonate in 1938 and 1939.

Wilson's objective to transform the world into one "made safe for democracy " had failed.

Moreover, his efforts to use American exceptionalism to convert his followers to a new approach to foreign policy also failed for the next two decades. Ironically, by the 1930s public reaction to Wilson's true transformational achievement of bringing the United States into World War I led to a virulent isolationism that complicated the situation Franklin Roosevelt inherited. The reaction produced the interwar period of retrenchment. Overly ambitious transformational objectives combined with overconfidence in an inspirational style ultimately proved counterproductive to the smooth creation of an American era.

The Second Phase: Entry into World War II

Franklin Delano Roosevelt not only was the longest serving American president but is one whom historians rank among the most important. Coming to power in the depths of the Great Depression, he launched a number of domestic reforms that may not alone have solved the economic crisis but are generally credited with transforming American politics and government. His inspirational style as a masterful actor and communicator illustrated that the distinction between style and substance can sometimes become blurred when we consider transformational leadership. But interestingly, when it came to foreign policy during his first two terms, Roosevelt's style was transactional rather than inspirational. Given the strong isolationist sentiment among his followers, he was very careful not to get too far ahead of his public. As Robert Dallek has written, "He never lost sight of the proposition that foreign policy in a democracy, especially one necessitating painful sacrifices, could not survive without a national consensus. . . . In response to the evolving world crisis in his second term, he remained in step with public opinion by waiting on events."[21] In style it is almost as if there were two Roosevelt presidencies in the 1930s.

On foreign policy Roosevelt had reasonable contextual intelligence, but more about Europe than Asia. He was a supporter of the League who had served in Wilson's Navy Department and had broad knowledge of Europe through travel. Not surprisingly, however, given the state of the economy in 1933, he came into office paying little attention to foreign policy, and one of his early actions was to reject the conclusions of an economic conference in London that Herbert Hoover had scheduled. He had no transformational objectives for foreign policy when he entered office. In line with American tradition, he allowed his State Department to focus on trade and on a good-neighbor policy for Latin America.

Hitler and Roosevelt were elected to office in the same year, but only gradually did the latter become aware of the threat Hitler posed. Even this slowly growing awareness of a change in the international context was well ahead of the rest of the country. In 1937 during the Spanish Civil War, Roosevelt gently and ambiguously suggested a quarantine on both sides, but while the strategic probe was useful to him, he publicly withdrew his toe from that water when the domestic politics proved it to be hot. During the crucial period 1936–38, Roosevelt's policy was to slow the drift to war and to avoid American involvement if war nonetheless occurred.[22] By the spring of 1938 he had come to believe that Germany had the capability to harm the United States, but "not until the Munich crisis ended his uncertainty about Hitler's intentions could he finally settle on a policy."[23]

In late 1938 Munich and Kristallnacht were the turning point in Roosevelt's personal views. While he publicly supported the Munich Agreement, he privately concluded that it was "impossible to work with Hitler in any meaningful way." He knew he had to change American foreign policy, but the task was daunting. In structural terms, it should not have been difficult. American power had increased, with the economy now representing nearly 26 percent of what the world produced in 1938.[24] Roosevelt wanted to use that economic power to depart from neutrality and bolster Britain and France, particularly in the production of aircraft. But the American people were unwilling to support policies to translate that underlying strength into political and military actions. In a series of Gallup polls conducted in 1936 and 1937, 70 percent of respondents believed it had been a mistake to enter World War I. In the spring and summer of 1940, no more than 10 percent of respondents said the United States should send its army abroad. Over the next year, support for a declaration of war increased to 23 percent—but even then, the vast majority of the public opposed it.[25] Americans did not share Roosevelt's perception of the Nazi threat. As late as 1940 American armed forces ranked seventeenth in size, with 300,000 soldiers, compared to Germany's 4 million and Britain's 1.6 million.

Not a single armored division existed, and half the navy's vessels dated back to World War I.[26]

What does a leader with transformational objectives do when his contextual intelligence discerns a slowly growing threat but his followers do not? As Roosevelt told his speechwriter Samuel Rosenman in 1938, "it's a terrible thing to look over your shoulder when you are trying to lead—and to find no one there."[27] Over the next three years, while Roosevelt adhered to a doctrine of nonintervention in public, his private concerns grew, and he undertook measures that could quietly support the allies and prepare the United States for a war when it came. Many of the steps, such as trading destroyers for British bases in the Caribbean or lend lease, in which aid to Britain was likened to a temporary loan of a garden hose to a neighbor, were presented to the American people as purely transactional. Others, such as basing troops in Iceland, were justified by stretching traditional terms about protecting the Western Hemisphere.

Roosevelt tried speeches and meetings, but after an hour-long appeal to senators in 1939 he was still unable to change the Neutrality Act. As he once put it, "If you ever sit here, you will learn that you cannot, just by shouting from the housetops, get what you want all the time."[28] A leader must always look over his or her shoulder and adjust speed in a democracy, but what can be done if the followers are marching in an opposite direction? One possibility is to create crises to help educate the public. Roosevelt tried to engineer a number of incidents at sea, even outright lying about the alleged attack of a German submarine upon the destroyer USS *Greer* in September 1941, but to little avail.

As the situation worsened, he began to use more inspirational rhetoric about freedom in the August 1941 Atlantic Charter that he signed with Churchill. But like Wilson in 1916, he ran his 1940 election campaign with the deceptive slogan that "your sons will not go to war."

In the end, Roosevelt's dilemma was solved by Japan's attack on Pearl Harbor and Hitler's mistake of declaring war on the United States in support of his Axis ally. After December 7, 1941, Roosevelt was able to unleash his full rhetorical capabilities and indulge his inspirational style in foreign policy. Some have suggested that Pearl Harbor was one of his engineered crises, but historians now agree that it was not.[29] The Japanese attack seems to have been produced in part by the ambiguity of the US oil embargo in the Pacific and a combination of Roosevelt's loose management style and inattentiveness to detail as midlevel officials implemented his policies. Many historians believe that Roosevelt did not actively seek war with Japan but intended "to slip the noose around Japan's neck and give it a jerk now and then."[30]

Japan regarded the oil embargo as a dire threat to their economy, but Roosevelt wanted the embargo to be an on-again, off-again signaling device. He was not attentive to the fact that the bureaucracy implemented it as a complete embargo. While some historians see a clever design to provoke war with Japan as a "back door" for entry into the European war, Roosevelt could not be sure that Hitler would come to the aid of Japan, and Roosevelt's handling of relations with Japan showed considerable ineptitude.[31] In the words of one historian, "Neither [Cordell] Hull nor the president managed to maintain control over the constantly growing and increasingly complex foreign policy bureaucracy. By losing control over the execution of policy, they lost control over the direction the nation moved."[32] In contrast to his knowledge of Europe, Roosevelt's contextual intelligence about Asia was not strong, but ironically it was Asia (and Hitler) that solved his dilemma of how to enter Hitler's war. In this sense, despite the tragedy of lives lost, Pearl Harbor was an element of luck for Roosevelt, and he had prepared to be able to use such an event if it happened. It allowed him to transform American foreign policy dramatically and ensured that the attitudes of the American public would be supportive of the new approach despite his previous failures to convert them away from isolationism in the 1930s.

THE THIRD PHASE: CONTAINMENT AND PERMANENT PRESENCE OVERSEAS

Harry S. Truman

Harry Truman could not have had a more different background from his predecessors who presided over the transformation of American foreign policy. While they had degrees from Harvard, Yale, and Princeton, the "little man with glasses" from Missouri never attended college and spent ten years working on his father's farm. While the two Roosevelts came into office with considerable contextual intelligence about foreign affairs, Truman's international experience was limited to brief service as an officer in France during World War I and as a senator. And while he also served for two and a half months as Roosevelt's vice president, Roosevelt never consulted him about such important issues as the atomic bomb, the Yalta Conference, or much else. In David McCulloch's words, Truman was "a nineteenth-century man,"[33] yet he made some of the most important foreign policy decisions of the twentieth century, both in establishing the grand strategy of containment that persisted for four decades and in creating domestic and international institutions. If Wilson and Roosevelt broke from tradition by sending large American armies overseas, Truman was pivotal by keeping them there. He moved foreign policy from "no entangling alliances" to a permanent presence abroad and a NATO alliance that lasted into the next century.

In structural terms, Truman inherited a world in 1945 where American power was unprecedented. Because of the uneven effects of World War II on various economies, the United States accounted for nearly half the world product. Unlike in the 1930s, victorious American armies were positioned in Europe and Asia, and the United States had sole possession of the new nuclear superweapon. But such power resources did not transfer automatically into a policy of primacy. While the Americans tried to gain diplomatic leverage from their atomic monopoly at the 1945 Potsdam Conference, and the military occupation of conquered German and Japan created new postwar facts on the ground, the democratic political pressures at home led to rapid demobilization of American armies, and the dominant political concerns were not about international primacy but about domestic employment and whether the postwar economy would relapse into depression. When a 1945 Gallup poll posed the question "What do you think is the most important problem facing the country during the next year?" jobs and strikes were the most frequently cited responses.[34] Yet American opinion was no longer isolationist. In October 1945, 71 percent of respondents believed it would be better for the future of the United States to take an active part in world affairs,[35] and surveys conducted by the National Opinion Research Center for the State Department reveal that between 1945 and 1956 the share of respondents who believed the United States should take an active role in the world never dipped below 70 percent.[36]

Truman did not come into office with transformational objectives, and he certainly did not have an inspirational style. On the contrary, he was a regular Wilsonian Democrat committed to implementing Roosevelt's "Grand Design" for a postwar order based on collective security bolstered by the realist device of "four [later five] policemen"—great powers ensconced as permanent members of a new UN Security Council. In June 1950, when the Soviets made the tactical error of boycotting the Security Council and thereby allowed collective security to work after North Korean armies crossed the 38th parallel into South Korea, Truman responded not as a careful strategist but in what Ernest May called "an axiomatic" reflection of his deepest beliefs.[37] He had learned the lessons of the 1930s and vowed not to allow aggression to go unanswered again.

Some critics cite Truman's dressing down of Vyacheslav Molotov during the Soviet foreign minister's first visit to the White House in April 1945 shortly after Truman became president as proof that he came into office with a Cold War orientation. But that incident reflected Truman's naïve American reaction to Soviet lies rather than a transformational objective. If anything, like Roosevelt, Truman underestimated Stalin's malevolent intentions and mistakenly compared him to Kansas City boss Tom Pendergast (in an example of simplistic mirror imaging rather than contextual empathy).[38] Even after George Kennan's long telegram from Moscow warned Washington about Soviet intentions, Truman tried to preserve Roosevelt's policy by asking trusted aide Clark Clifford to poll the views of people in the government. When Clifford's report reinforced Kennan in the summer of 1946, Truman ordered that it be restricted to ten copies and locked up.[39] Robert Dallek calls the year and a half between the end of the war and the Truman Doctrine "one of the most difficult and confusing periods in U.S. diplomatic history . . . [as] Americans gyrated between hopes of peaceful cooperation and fears of all-out strife."[40] It was not until February 1947, in the context of British withdrawal in the eastern Mediterranean, that he agreed to the great transformational steps of doctrine, followed months later by the Marshall Plan and then creation of the North Atlantic Treaty Organization (NATO) in 1949.

Was Truman a transformational leader in responding to this newly perceived context, or did he only ratify the views of the "wise men" around him? Was he a mere McKinley? After all, Truman was not a charismatic leader nor a great communicator. Though he believed in heroic leaders from his personal reading of history, he was never sure he measured up. Like many government actions, the great decisions of the third phase of the creation of American primacy were to some extent collective. Undersecretary of State Dean Acheson and Senator Arthur Vandenberg framed the issue at crucial White House meetings in 1947.

George Marshall gave the famous Harvard commencement address that later led to his eponymous plan, and Truman revered Marshall. But Marshall was the beneficiary rather than the strategic initiator of his plan, and, as Isaacson and Thomas have observed, even the famous wise men—Dean Acheson, Averell Harriman, Robert Lovett, John McCloy, George Kennan, and Charles Bohlen—each had blind spots and shortcomings. "No single one could have guided the country to its new role as world power." Yet collectively they "brought to the immense task just the right mixture of vision and practicality, aggressiveness and patience."[41] In this sense Truman showed that transformational leadership in terms of setting new objectives can be collective, and that presidents deserve credit (and blame) for the selection and orchestration of their subordinates.

But what was Truman's role? Was he a mere conduit for others as he had largely been when he agreed to drop the atomic bomb on Hiroshima a little over three months after came into office? Such a picture underestimates Truman's leadership in several ways. First, it misses his ability to select and command the respect of the impressive team he appointed. Second, it underrates his on-the-job learning and his ability to develop his contextual intelligence while in office. Third, it misses his willingness to take tough decisions, such as standing up to Marshall on the creation of Israel, firing MacArthur, and resisting the use of nuclear weapons after the Korean War bogged down. Similarly, Truman resisted full funding for the hawkish document NSC 68 that Paul Nitze and others prepared—until the North Korean invasion changed the context.

Above all, it misses Truman's Wilsonian view of American exceptionalism and the difference that made to the way the doctrine of containment was formulated.[42] As John Gaddis has pointed out, it was Truman's decision to follow Acheson and Vandenberg's advice to frame containment as a defense of free people everywhere rather than an issue of the balance of power in the eastern Mediterranean. George Kennan was dismayed by this militarization and ideological expansion of his original concept. Some analysts complain that Truman's open-ended, universal commitment led eventually to the disaster of the Vietnam War, but that is too simple. Truman provided aid to Tito's Yugoslavia, and in Asia he followed Marshall's advice and did not become involved in what would have been a losing effort to protect Chiang Kai-shek's nationalist regime from the advancing communist forces in China.

Moreover, Truman's emphasis on the values embodied in his doctrine and in the Marshall Plan also contributed to the institutionalization of the Atlantic alliance. The liberal nature of American primacy made it more stable. In the words of a Norwegian scholar, America succeeded in maintaining the allegiance of postwar Europe because it was "an empire by integration."[43] In any event, it was Truman's interpretation of the objectives of containment that guided foreign policy as the United States responded to the new structure of bipolarity after World War II. Truman entered office with neither transformational objectives nor an inspirational style. His style remained transactional, but through on-the-job learning he became a transformational foreign policy leader.

Dwight D. Eisenhower

The key decisions in the third phase of the creation of American primacy—containing the Soviet Union and maintaining a permanent presence abroad—were made by Truman, but they were consolidated into a prudent and sustainable system by his successor, Dwight Eisenhower. Truman left office with very low approval ratings, and the new American foreign policy was far from consolidated. The Wallace wing of the Democratic Party believed Truman was too uncompromising with the Soviet Union, and the Republican Party was divided between a more aggressive group that attacked "the cowardly college of containment" and Robert Taft's isolationist wing, which wanted to reduce American commitment abroad. In fact, Eisenhower did not originally intend to run for president but decided to do so when he feared that Taft might get the nomination in 1952.

Like Truman, Eisenhower came from a humble midwestern background, but his opportunity to attend West Point and his distinguished career in the army in World War II gave him a greater contextual intelligence about international affairs than any previous president had. There would be no need for on-the-job learning. The famous White House Solarium exercise of 1953 was less to educate Eisenhower than for the leader to educate his cabinet and close staff. By framing three options of rollback, containment, and deterrence, Ike fended off the two wings of his party (isolationists and advocates of rollback) and not surprisingly came down in favor of the middle option. He even used George Kennan to present the case for the

containment option. Secretary of State John Foster Dulles
had refused a new assignment for Kennan. "Dulles' bluster
had long made Eisenhower uneasy, but in a Republican
Party still dominated by isolationists and McCarthyites, he
seemed the only plausible possibility to run the Department of State. Despite the president's military background,
it was not his habit to discipline subordinates: instead he
sought to educate his secretary of state and others within
his administration about the probable risks, costs, and consequences of a more aggressive strategy." As Gaddis puts
it, Ike used Kennan "to liberate Eisenhower from the 'liberation' strategy to which Dulles had tried to commit him
during the 1952 campaign."[44]

Like Truman, Eisenhower came into office without
transformational objectives. He specifically sought status
quo and incremental objectives, and he was a transactional
leader in both methods and style. Eisenhower's contribution was to consolidate the doctrine of containment and
make it sustainable by a set of prudent judgments. Over
eight years in office, he avoided land wars in Korea and
Vietnam that transformational advocates of rollback (or
even less skilled incremental leaders) might have entered;
cut overseas spending to support the domestic economy;
and strengthened America's new alliances with Europe
and Japan. During that period the world economy—and
the economies of crucial US allies—grew impressively. He
was willing to negotiate with the Soviet Union and exercised great prudence at the time of the Soviet intervention
in Hungary in 1956. While he relied on nuclear threats of
massive retaliation to deter the Soviet Union and to save
spending on expensive land forces, he was simultaneously

very careful to reinforce the new nuclear taboo by resisting those who advocated the use of nuclear weapons against North Korea and China.

Eisenhower managed a broad public consensus on foreign policy. Ole R. Holsti argues that "if the term 'internationalist foreign policy consensus' was ever a valid description of the domestic bases of American foreign policy it would appear to have been most applicable to the period between the traumas of the Korean and Vietnam wars."[45] For example, in 1956, 59 percent of Republicans, 58 percent of Democrats, and 58 percent of Independents approved of foreign aid to help stop communism.[46] When asked by Gallup in the summer of 1954, a 62 percent majority considered themselves internationalist (17 percent considered themselves isolationist).[47] In a separate poll conducted that same summer, a large majority (76 percent) noted they approved of the United Nations.[48] Communism abroad was foremost on the minds of most Americans. When Gallup asked in the summer of 1955, "What do you regard as the biggest issue, or problem, facing the Government in Washington today?" 48 percent of respondents claimed "foreign policy problems, working out a peace, dealing with Russia, Red China."[49] But public opinion was not supportive of sending troops to Indochina. An overwhelming majority (72 percent) disapproved of sending American soldiers to take part in the fighting.[50]

Eisenhower had a unique style of leadership. He often "led from behind" with gentle persuasion rather than command. Despite, or perhaps because of, his military background, he had a good understanding of soft power, but he

exercised it more in personal relations than as a public orator in the fashion of Wilson or the two Roosevelts. As Fred
Greenstein has described, Eisenhower's "hidden-hand presidency" combined a visible monarchical style with an invis-
ible prime ministerial role. While Secretary of State Dulles
sounded rhetorical alarms, Eisenhower remained firmly in
control of policy. At home he consolidated and improved
Truman's institutional changes, such as the National Security Council (NSC) process. Ike had superb organizational
skills. He used the NSC to manage information and policy
flows, but also to educate his top officials. But the cost of
this low-key transactional style was sometimes a failure to
educate the public on issues like civil rights and the spuri-
ous missile gap.

Ike was not transformational in objectives or inspirational in style, but he understood the limits of American
power and managed crises well. For example, he coined
the unfortunate and misleading metaphor of dominoes
falling in Southeast Asia, but he had the contextual intelligence that helped him avoid letting the metaphor suck
him into a major intervention in Vietnam because it would
swallow up our troops "by the divisions." Having stated
that Indochina must be held and proclaimed a domino
theory, Eisenhower risked a loss of credibility, and the
decision was not easy for him.[51] Lyndon Johnson, who
lacked Eisenhower's understanding of international affairs, did not avoid this trap. The result of Ike's prudence
was eight years of peace and prosperity. An incremental
president with a transactional style can have a very effective foreign policy, and Eisenhower's consolidation of

containment completed the midcentury transformation of American foreign policy that was crucial to the creation of the American era.

THE FOURTH PHASE:
AMERICA BECOMES THE SOLE SUPERPOWER

The end of the Cold War in the late 1980s and the end of the Soviet Union in 1991 left the United States in an unprecedented position as the sole superpower with global reach and no effective countervailing balancer. The structure of world politics had indeed changed dramatically. But few observers saw it coming, much less planned it. After the setback of the Vietnam War and its economic and political aftermath, many observers believed that the United States was in decline. In 1979 *Businessweek* displayed a cover picture of the Statue of Liberty weeping and proclaimed that the colossus was "clearly facing a decay of power."[52] A respected academic observed, "Under the impact of events that brought the last decade to a close and ushered in the 1980s, the fact of America's decline has become a commonplace."[53] As noted in chapter 1, Nixon and Kissinger had believed that the Soviet Union was beginning to surpass the United States in the bipolar competition, and they had turned to détente and an opening to China as tools to cope. Paul Nitze and other alarmists created a Committee on the Present Danger to warn against growing Soviet strength. Yet the erosion of the bipolar structure of world politics did not produce the Soviet supremacy that pessimists feared or the multipolarity that most expected. Instead it produced an unexpected unipolarity. Two very different Republicans presided over these changes: Ronald Reagan and his vice president and successor, George H. W. Bush.

Ronald Reagan

Reagan's leadership presents a series of paradoxes. He had serious deficiencies in his cognitive knowledge, but superb emotional effectiveness. Like Franklin Roosevelt, his performance suggests that there are instances of leadership where "style is substance." Reagan restored American self-confidence after the difficult decade of the 1970s when some establishment figures were questioning whether the country was governable under its existing constitution. Despite acknowledging his cognitive weaknesses, a sober journal like the *Economist* called him one of most consequential presidents of twentieth century and concluded that "this champion of simplicity was himself surprisingly hard to make sense of."[54]

Reagan's leadership skills included the ability to present a vision that was attractive to American followers by stressing the "moral clarity" of good versus evil. He believed strongly in ideas that were simple but not simplistic, and as he told his speechwriter Peggy Noonan, "There is no question that I am an idealist which is another way of saying I am an American."[55] He had the best ability to communicate it to the public of any president since Franklin Roosevelt. Like Roosevelt, Reagan had emotional intelligence and great ability as an actor, as well as impressive Machiavellian political skills. He was very good at bargaining and pragmatic about forming coalitions. He would talk tough but then bargain. Rhetoric about an evil empire did not prevent him from reaching agreements with Gorbachev, despite the contrary advice of some of his advisors.

In addition to his deficient knowledge base, Reagan's weakness was in his organizational capacity. While he was not a prisoner of his staff, he depended heavily on those he appointed, and after delegation he was inattentive to a fault. Unlike Ike, Reagan played the monarch but without the hidden hand. He failed to understand the implications of the Donald Regan/James Baker switch of positions between secretary of the treasury and White House chief of staff in 1985 that set the scene for a scandal that nearly destroyed his presidency. Despite six NSC advisors over eight years, he was never able to manage the George Shultz versus Caspar Weinberger battles that prevented smooth relations between the State and Defense Departments.

Failure to monitor highly risky appointees like William Casey, John Poindexter, and Oliver North nearly led to the destruction of Reagan's presidency in the Iran/Contra scandal, which involved trading arms for hostages and misusing the proceeds for covert action in Central America. As for contextual intelligence, Reagan saw the big picture in simplified terms of his values, which gave him a strong sense of direction and conviction about his objectives, but he was unable to master all the details relevant to implementation.[56] In the words of David Abshire, who helped to clean up the Iran/Contra problem in 1987, "In Ronald Reagan, perhaps, the United States has never had a president with such great talent for transformational and so little interest in transactional leadership."[57]

Reagan was transformational in his objectives and inspirational in his style, but it is debatable how transformational he was in causing the outcomes he sought. His initial objectives were to change the détente orientation that had characterized containment since the Nixon administration and get tougher with the Soviet Union. In this he succeeded, though Jack Matlock, an important advisor on Soviet affairs, says that Reagan's initial objectives did not include rollback or regime change.[58] Reagan did not buy into the status quo of the Cold War, and his combination of a rhetorical offensive plus a military buildup was designed to put pressure on an ailing Soviet Union. In this he succeeded, but he deserves most credit for being able to shift to negotiations. He intuited Gorbachev's willingness to bargain (well before other members of his administration) and then was able to establish a good working relationship.

At the same time, one of Reagan's strongest transformational objectives was to rid the world of nuclear weapons, and on this, of course, he failed. Ironically, he made progress on the nuclear issue at the Reykjavik summit but failed when he refused Gorbachev's request to constrain Strategic Defense Initiative (SDI) testing to the laboratory. In this instance Reagan failed in part because of his cognitive misunderstanding. Many members of the administration saw SDI as a bargaining chip, but Reagan really believed it would work as a shield as promised and thus refused limits that would not have mattered seriously to its development.

Was Reagan transformational in bringing about the end of the Cold War? His actions contributed to the outcome, in part through his military buildup, which put stress on the Soviet system, and later his willingness to bargain with Gorbachev. But Reagan actions were not nearly as crucial as those of Gorbachev. Gorbachev was truly transformational in his effects, though not in achieving his objective, which was to reform rather than destroy the Soviet Union. Without the unintended consequences of his efforts, the Soviet Union might have limped along for another decade or more. Ultimately, however, the deepest causes of Soviet collapse were structural: the decline of communist ideology and the failure of the Soviet economy. This would have happened even without Gorbachev or Reagan. Behind this was the decline in the Soviet economy, reflecting the diminished ability of the Soviet central planning system to respond to change in the global information economy. Stalin had created a system of centralized economic direction that emphasized heavy metal and smokestack industries. It was inflexible—all thumbs and no fingers. As the economist Joseph Schumpeter pointed out, capitalism is creative destruction, a way of responding flexibly to major waves of technological change. At the end of the twentieth century, the major technological change of the third industrial revolution was the growing role of information as the scarcest resource in an economy. The Soviet system was particularly inept at handling information. The deep secrecy of its political system meant that the flow of information was slow and cumbersome. As Foreign Minister Eduard Shevardnadze told his officials, "You and I represent a great country that in the last 15 years has been more and more losing its position as one of the leading industrially developed nations."[59]

Ronald Reagan had the intuition and political skills to see Gorbachev as a bargaining partner, and that helped to account for part of the timing, if not a major part of the causation, of the end of the Cold War. If Yuri Andropov, a noted Soviet hard-liner, had not died of kidney disease, or alternatively if Gorbachev had come to power as general secretary of the Communist Party five years earlier when Jimmy Carter was president, Reagan's strategy and causal role would not have mattered. Reagan was lucky that Gorbachev was in the deck of cards that was dealt to him. His intuition and bargaining skills allowed him to contribute toward his transformational objective, but while he deserves credit for skillful handling of Gorbachev, his larger role in the causation of the end of the Cold War was not the key to the transformation. The basic causes were structural, and the proximate causes were Gorbachev's policies of perestroika, glasnost, and new thinking in foreign policy.

George H. W. Bush

The final dissolution of the Soviet Union occurred in December 1991 under the presidency of George H. W. Bush. Like Franklin Roosevelt, Bush had a patrician background and an Ivy League education. But unlike Roosevelt or Reagan, Bush was neither a great communicator nor an accomplished actor, and that gave him a very transactional style. Like Eisenhower, though at a different level, Bush was a distinguished combat veteran, but his upbringing made him reticent about self-promotion. Also like Eisenhower, he was among the most experienced men in international affairs to occupy the presidency, and this gave him excellent contextual intelligence. He also shared an important ability to pick able subordinates, and to organize an effective national security process. These skills plus good emotional intelligence served him well in his adept management of the dismantling of the Cold War, as well as the creation of a coalition that revived UN collective security (for the first time since 1950) in the 1991 Gulf War. At the same time, these traits limited Bush's ability to use his office to educate the public. While he spoke about a "new world order" (a phrase borrowed from Gorbachev) and a democratic peace, he never articulated or communicated these concepts as a vision that could capture public opinion.

Although Bush was incremental in his objectives, he presided successfully over a major transformation of the world. When the Bush administration entered office, it was skeptical of Reagan's infatuation with Gorbachev and cautious in picking up where Reagan left off. In particular, it did not share Reagan's nuclear abolitionism. But after the Malta summit in 1989, Bush demonstrated extraordinary skill in managing the unification of Germany within NATO (against the advice of many advisors and allies) and the eventual peaceful dismantlement of the Soviet Union in 1991.

Few people predicted in 1989 that within a year the two German states would be reunited, much less that unity would occur within NATO. But 1989–90 was one of those moments of rare fluidity in international politics that bubble up out of domestic changes, and two transformational leaders with different objectives, Gorbachev and German Chancellor Helmut Kohl, took advantage of that fluidity to change the world. Bush made an important bet in backing his friend Kohl while skillfully handling the relationship with Gorbachev. In that sense he contributed greatly to the transformation. But some historians have asked whether he could have made a bigger bet that might have avoided the alienation of Russia. In the words of one, "Bush had told the American electorate that he was not enamored of grand visions and he remained true to his word. What resulted from his foreign policy leadership as a result was by no means unfortunate, but it was not ideal. He defended the interests of the United States but . . . the decision to extend prefabricated settlement architecture only to Eastern Europe, not Russia, seemed a throwback to an earlier era."[60]

Zbigniew Brzezinski and others have praised Bush for his skillful management of a transformational moment in history but faulted him for failing to set more transformational objectives in his foreign policy. Bush is famous for saying "I don't do the vision thing," and despite pleas from his advisors he was reluctant to follow Reagan's ambitious objectives or rhetorical style. Bush's vision of a new world order was that of a realist, though he borrowed the language of UN collective security when it could work at the end of Cold War. In other words, a seventy-year-old Wilsonian vision was the default option. He failed to develop a new or broader vision that set new objectives. Brzezinski faults him for not seeing the potential for a vision that promoted democracy in Russia; not pushing harder for a solution to the Israel-Palestine dispute that roiled the Middle East and the Muslim world; and not taking a stronger position on North Korean and South Asian nuclear proliferation.[61]

Administration defenders question whether anyone could have solved these problems. They note that Bush (and his able secretary of state, James Baker) made a big push on Israel-Palestine at the 1992 Madrid Conference and say that more might have been tackled if Bush had been able to win a second term. Instead Bush emphasized prudence, except on Germany, where his objective of unification was more transformational than that of a number of his aides and allies. Moreover, he had to balance many changes at the same time: the fall of the Berlin Wall, nuclear issues, Iraq's invasion of Kuwait, the Tiananmen Square repression, civil war in Yugoslavia, and others. Bush's objectives were based on realist prudence. The decline of the Soviet Union and the rise of Europe created a situation where the administration could look at the collapse of Yugoslavia and conclude that the United States had "no dog in that fight." This position was not based on lack of contextual intelligence or ignorance of the situation, but on clear priorities. Bush's objective was to preside over extraordinary and favorable external change without dropping any of the balls that were in the air.

According to his staff, Bush's leadership style was "restless but unassuming, at once both relaxed and reserved. . . . His style with foreign leaders bordered on the indirect, but sooner or later he would make his point. His managerial style was equally disciplined. He would discuss issues individually with top subordinates, clearly conveying the principles he cared about. But he would almost never visibly intervene in subcabinet or even some cabinet-level policy discussions." Bush surrounded himself with "people who shared his penchant for low-key rhetoric and careful attention to details . . . who could get along and keep their egos in check" and keep him constantly informed.[62] His political organizational skills were impressive, and his National Security advisor, Brent Scowcroft, and deputy, Robert Gates, were renowned for running a fair and prudent process.

Bush was not transformational in his objectives or inspirational in his style, but he presided successfully over a major structural transformation from a bipolar to a unipolar world. If any of the balls that Bush was juggling had been dropped, the consequences could have been disastrous for the world and for the consolidation of American primacy. In such circumstances, Bush might ask the critics who complain that he presided over a transformation but did not sufficiently adjust his incremental objectives to build on it whether it is better to have an incremental leader with prudence or a transformational leader with an unusual vision. I will revisit this question when I compare the two Bush presidencies in the concluding chapter.

How Effective Were Transformational and Inspirational Leaders?

Leadership theorists tend to assume that transformational leaders are "better." As noted earlier, that can mean more effective or more ethical or both. I will address ethics in the next chapter, so the question here relates to the effectiveness of the eight leaders who presided over the creation of the American era, and I will disaggregate the term transformational to distinguish both objectives and style. As the table 2.1 illustrates, there are at least three dimensions of what is called transformational leadership, and in terms of style, most leaders mix transformational (i.e., inspirational) and transactional styles.

TABLE 2.1. EFFECTIVENESS OF TRANSFORMATIONAL
AND INSPIRATIONAL LEADERSHIP

	Tranformational objectives?	Inspirational style?	Tranformational outcome (within a decade)?
T. Roosevelt	Yes	Yes, mixed	No
Taft	No	No	No
Wilson	After 1917	Yes	Yes
F. Roosevelt	After 1938	Yes, mixed	Yes
Truman	After 1947	No	Yes
Eisenhower	No	No	No
Reagan	Yes	Yes	Yes
Bush	No (except Germany)	No	Yes

Of the eight leaders who were president during the four positive phases in the creation of the American era, five were transformational in their objectives, and three (Taft, Eisenhower, and Bush) were mostly incremental in their objectives. Two were primarily inspirational in style (Wilson and Reagan), and four primarily transactional (Taft, Truman, Eisenhower, and Bush). In terms of world outcomes, five were successful in contributing to significant change by the end of their administrations (Wilson, F. Roosevelt, Truman, Reagan, and Bush), and Franklin Roosevelt, Truman, and Reagan were also able to transform the attitudes of their followers by the end of their administrations. At best this is a mixed scorecard with only three who held transformational objectives (F. Roosevelt, Truman, Reagan) contributing to major changes in America's position in the world as measured by the outcome a decade after they served. And of those who were primarily inspirational in their foreign policy style, one failed and one succeeded. Moreover, Eisenhower and Bush, who were both primarily status quo in objectives and transactional in style, are often credited with very effective contributions to the creation of the American era. While they did not set out to change foreign policy, their extraordinary contextual intelligence and prudent management avoided crises that might well have derailed the creation of the American era.

If the United States had succumbed to the temptations of isolationism, rollback, or use of nuclear weapons in the 1950s, or if the unification of Germany and the disintegration of the Soviet Union had been accompanied by violence and loss of control of nuclear weapons in the Bush era, the outcomes for the creation of the American era would have looked very different. Nonevents can be as important to an effective foreign policy as events. Thus the evidence is far from supportive of the proposition that transformational leaders are necessarily more effective than incremental leaders or that an inspirational style is more effective when it comes to foreign policy.

Success depends more on other variables than whether a leader has a transformational or status quo objective and an inspirational or transactional style. These variables include changes in context, learning by the public, and other traits of the leaders (as described in table 1.2). For example, if Woodrow Wilson had possessed better emotional intelligence, he might have been less stubborn and more willing to compromise with the Senate and allowed the ratification of the League of Nations. While this stubbornness was partly a result of poor health after his stroke, he had demonstrated a similar emotional rigidity at earlier stages in his career.[63] If Ronald Reagan had had better organizational skills, he might have avoided the Iran/Contra scandal and pressed further in his dealings with Gorbachev. If Bush had been a better communicator or been brought up to be less modest, might he have set higher goals at the end of the Cold War? We cannot know, but at least we can avoid falling into the easy assumption that transformational is synonymous with more effective foreign policy leadership.

Counterfactual History

We can also test how strong the effects of leadership were by imagining what might have happened if these eight leaders had not become president. Some people object to this as "iffy" history and point out that the number of possible counterfactuals is infinite and that history is rarely linear. That is why good counterfactual history must be more than just spinning out imaginative scenarios. To meet the valid concerns of the critics, one should discipline counterfactuals by limiting them to those that are proximate in time, that hold most other things constant, and that do not stretch credulity too far. We must be wary of piling one counterfactual on top of another in the same thought experiment. Such multiple counterfactuals are confusing because too many things are being changed at once, and we are unable to judge the accuracy of the exercise by a careful examination of its real historical parts.[64] To meet these criteria, I will speculate about what might have happened if the leader had not become president, and the most plausible contender had been in his place instead.

Theodore Roosevelt

If McKinley had survived the assassination attempt and Roosevelt had not become president, America's involvement in the global balance of power through mediating great power disputes might have been delayed by a decade. On the other hand, policy in the Caribbean, an isthmus canal (though perhaps not in Panama), a continuing rapprochement with Great Britain, and the Japanese colonization of Korea would likely have occurred in any case. Roosevelt's good contextual intelligence allowed him to see gradual changes in the global balance well ahead of his public followers, and his energetic leadership traits allowed him to speed up the involvement of the United States in global politics somewhat, but structural forces would have produced much the same outcome within a decade or so. For all his vision and ebullient style, Teddy Roosevelt did not add much to what would have been predicted by structural explanations alone.

William Howard Taft

If Roosevelt had broken his earlier promise and chosen to run for a third term in 1908, or if Taft had accepted the earlier offer of appointment to the Supreme Court, he would not have become president. American economic power would have continued to grow, and a third term might have allowed Roosevelt to continue to push for a greater global role for the United States. But Taft's incremental objectives tended to limit his foreign policy primarily to a traditional focus. Had he been more transformational in objectives and inspirational in style, America's global role might have advanced as if there had been a third Roosevelt term. As Willard Straight, a contemporary American diplomat, observed about Taft's lack of success in China in 1911, America was not "yet well enough equipped or sufficiently experienced to deal in a masterful manner with the problems which confront the country now embarking on its career as a world power."[65] Neither Taft nor a hypothesized third-term Roosevelt was in a position to back open-door diplomacy in Asia by credible force. Taft's leadership style may have somewhat slowed down the evolution of the American era, but structure still explains more.

Woodrow Wilson

If Roosevelt had not run as an independent in the three-way presidential race of 1912, it is likely that Taft would have been reelected.[66] Since events in Europe in 1914 unfolded independently of events in the United States, the dilemma of American participation in World War I would have arisen in any case as a result of structural forces. In the face of German submarines sinking American ships, and with pressure from the Roosevelt wing of the Republican Party, it is likely that a second-term President Taft (despite his predilections for arbitration) would have been drawn into the allied side of the war, and perhaps sooner. But without Woodrow Wilson, American participation would not have been wrapped in the morality of American exceptionalism with the fourteen points and the Covenant of the League of Nations.

The modest type of league that was acceptable to Taft, Roosevelt, and even Henry Cabot Lodge might have permitted a more active American place in global politics, though it is an open question whether American participation in the League would have helped a more stable international order to become sufficiently rooted in the 1920s that it might have been able to cope with the Fascist foreign policies that were a product of much stronger domestic economic and social forces in the 1930s. But a more limited and gradual entry into the balance of power might have produced less disillusion and less intensity in the public isolationist reactions in the interwar period. Because Wilson used traditional American exceptionalism to justify the entry into the war, he succeeded in his short-term transformational change of sending troops to fight in Europe, but this might have occurred under another president such as Teddy Roosevelt or Taft.

In the longer term, however, Wilson left a legacy of ideas and values that became an important part of future American foreign policy discourse, as I will discuss in the next chapter. Ironically, Wilson also affected the foreign policies of the four administrations that followed his, but like Gorbachev in the Soviet Union decades later, the changes he wrought were not in the intended direction of his objectives. Wilson's leadership changed things in ways that cannot fully be explained by structural arguments, though not on the whole in the ways he intended.

Franklin Roosevelt

When Franklin Roosevelt ran for an unprecedented third term as president in 1940, he was fortunate to be opposed by Wendell Wilkie, an eastern establishment Republican who shared his internationalist views. The novelist Philip Roth has imagined an alternative scenario in which the aviation hero and isolationist Charles Lindbergh is drafted and accepts the Republican nomination in 1940.[67] If a Lindbergh-like president had been more accommodating to Japan and not imposed an oil embargo, Japan might have chosen a different path of attack, such as Siberia, for its aggression, and without Pearl Harbor it would have been much more difficult for the United States to enter Hitler's War. It is worth remembering that Japan considered various options in 1941, and Admiral Yamamoto, who led the strike on Pearl Harbor, recommended against it.[68]

Moreover, Roosevelt was fortunate that Hitler decided to strengthen the Axis by declaring war on the United States. As Roosevelt's aide Harry Hopkins said on December 7, 1941, "The Japanese attack was a Godsend, for by no other means could the country have been brought into the war without serious internal disunity."[69] This suggests that Roosevelt's crucial role in bringing America into the war was a product of luck more than skill, but his preparation to take advantage of luck depended on his contextual intelligence and measures such as rearmament, selective service, and aid to Britain. After 1938 he saw Nazi Germany as a threat to the United States and tried to make America as ready for war as public opinion would allow.[70] His actions in the North Atlantic have even been described as an "undeclared war."[71] In this instance, it was Roosevelt's transformational preparation to take advantage of events in the case of war that was crucial.

Structuralists may argue that no matter who was president, structural forces and the threat from Hitler would have brought the United States into the war within a few years in any event. But Bruce Russett has laid out a skeptical view of US entry into World War II. Using realist assumptions, he argues that after Hitler's mistake of invading the Soviet Union in June 1941, the United States would have been better off letting Russia and Germany fight to a stalemate, and that "the battle of Stalingrad in late 1942 marked the final visible blunting of Hitler's drive to the East."[72] The Americans would have developed an atomic bomb by 1946 or 1947, and the Germans lagged far behind. By entering the war and setting an objective of unconditional surrender, Roosevelt ensured that the Soviets would enter Central Europe to fill the vacuum at the end of the fighting. Whether Russet's counterfactual is correct is less relevant than the fact that Roosevelt never entertained it. A staunch anticommunist isolationist might have given it more credence. Having Roosevelt in the White House rather than a Lindbergh-type isolationist had causal effects that would not be predicted by structural explanations alone.

Harry Truman

To continue our counterfactual speculation, suppose that Roosevelt had been in better health and lived out his full fourth term. Vice President Truman would never have become president and would not have mattered. Roosevelt would have dropped the atomic bomb, and we know that he suffered from some of the same illusions about Stalin that afflicted Truman's early years. Indeed, Truman may have caught the affliction in part from his predecessor. "Roosevelt apparently had forgotten, if indeed he ever knew, that in Stalin's eyes he was not that different from Hitler, both of them being heads of powerful capitalist states whose long term ambitions clashed with those of the Kremlin."[73] Some analysts believe that had Roosevelt lived, his ability to manipulate seemingly intractable situations could have led to a division of spheres of influence through cautious collaboration rather than "an all-out militarized competition checked only by the threat of nuclear annihilation." They argue that "the personality of a Harry Truman . . . made a decisive and lasting difference."[74] But we also know that shortly before his death, Roosevelt was beginning to have second thoughts about the Soviets and the prospects for his grand design. If so, the early days of the Cold War might not have been very different.

But suppose instead that Roosevelt had chosen to keep Henry Wallace as vice president for his fourth term. Given Wallace's strong preference for accommodation with the Soviets, American officialdom and public opinion might have been much slower to react, and Kennan's famous long telegram might have had less effect. If Stalin would have continued to probe when he encountered a weak reaction, the situation could have led to even more dangerous crises than those that occurred. In this counterfactual, Truman's leadership affected the timing of the American response to Soviet probes, as well as the particular American moral tone of Truman's rather than Kennan's (much less

Wallace's) brand of containment. As biographer Alonzo Hamby has argued, "In the end Truman's temperament was more important than his intellect, and Kennan never quite grasped the need for a guiding cause in American foreign policy."[75] Having Truman rather than Wallace as president had causal effects not fully predictable by structural explanations alone.

Dwight Eisenhower

If Robert Taft had run against and defeated Adlai Stevenson in 1952, there would have been no Eisenhower consolidation of the containment strategy and less permanent American presence overseas. Taft would have presided over a fractious Republican Party with McCarthyite China hawks eager for rollback of communism in Asia and isolationists like Senator Bricker and others trying to reduce American commitments in Europe and to the United Nations. It is hard to know how these tensions within the Republican Party would have played out, but it is less likely that the Truman legacy would have been consolidated in the manner that Eisenhower made possible. Eisenhower's stature as a war hero gave him great authority with the American public, and his impressive knowledge of international affairs gave him the contextual intelligence to avoid the use of nuclear weapons in Asia or to become involved in the ground war in Vietnam when the French appealed for help at Dien Bien Phu in 1954. Again, the presence of Eisenhower rather than Taft in the White House had effects that might not have been predictable by structural explanations alone.

Ronald Reagan

Jimmy Carter had a run of bad luck before the election of 1980, including the Soviet invasion of Afghanistan and the failure of the secret mission to rescue the American embassy personnel held hostage in Iran. Even so, early in the campaign it looked as if Reagan might not defeat Carter. If Carter had been reelected, would there have been the recovery of American self-confidence that was encouraged by the optimistic vision and inspirational style Ronald Reagan communicated? Or if Reagan had not survived the assassination attempt in 1981 and Bush had become president, would Bush have had the intuitive feel for Gorbachev's willingness to bargain? Initially Bush was skeptical of Gorbachev, with some key figures in the administration considering him "Andropov in a $900 suit." On the other hand, if Gorbachev had come to power during Carter's presidency, Carter might have found the interlocutor he sought for his foreign policy changes. In any event, as suggested above, the counterfactuals suggest that Reagan did play a secondary transformative role in ending the Cold War, but not nearly as much as Gorbachev. Like Roosevelt and Pearl Harbor, Reagan was lucky in the hand he was dealt, but his good leadership skills prepared him to play it well. Structural explanations probably account for much of the ending of the Cold War, but Reagan's leadership made a difference in the timing.

George H. W. Bush

Finally, we can imagine that in 1988 the early lead that Michael Dukakis had in the polls held up, and he defeated Bush for the presidency. In policy terms Dukakis would

have been even more forthcoming in trying to negotiate
with Gorbachev. There would have been no return to Cold
War or to isolationism, so the larger outlines of American
policy would have been the same. Moreover, given the internal economic and political problems that Gorbachev faced
and exacerbated by his futile efforts at reform, it is likely
that the Soviet Union would have collapsed in roughly the
same time frame since the changes depended more on Gorbachev than on American actions. The great unknowns,
however, are the dogs that did not bark. Would Dukakis,
with little experience in foreign affairs, have had the contextual intelligence and been able to sidestep the potential
crises as skillfully as Bush with his years of preparation for
the task? And would he have been prepared to manage the
Gulf War as successfully as Bush did? The answer cannot
be found solely in structural explanations. Even when a
situation like 1989–91 is determined by large-scale historical forces, many outcomes are possible. As a former Soviet
foreign minister observed, "'It was not that placid. There
were a lot of nerve-wracking situations in Moscow.' And
not only in Moscow."[76]

In surveying these speculative but plausible counterfactual exercises, it seems clear that most of these eight leaders
made a difference both in the timing and in the particular
characteristics of the creation of the American era. Would
structural forces have brought about the same American
era under different leaders? Theodore Roosevelt affected
mostly timing, but not very much. Taft slightly delayed
change, but not significantly. Wilson brought American
forces to fight in Europe, but that might have occurred
anyway under another leader. Where Wilson made a big

difference was in the American moral tone of his justification, and, counterproductively, in his stubborn insistence on all or nothing for involvement in the League of Nations. As for Franklin Roosevelt, it is at least debatable whether structural forces would have brought the United States into World War II under a conservative isolationist before it was too late, and Roosevelt's framing of the threat from Hitler and his preparations for taking advantage of his luck were crucial. Structural bipolarity set the framework for the Cold War, but a Wallace presidency might have changed the style of the American response and the timing of the response to its onset, and a Robert Taft or Douglas MacArthur presidency might have disrupted the relatively smooth consolidation of the containment system over which Eisenhower presided. At the end of the century, structural forces caused the erosion of the Soviet superpower, and Gorbachev speeded up the timing of Soviet collapse, but Reagan's defense buildup and his skill in negotiation and Bush's skill in managing crises were important to the final outcome in the creation of the American system.

Is there a plausible narrative in which, owing to different presidential leadership, America would not have developed primacy by the end of the twentieth century? Perhaps if Franklin Roosevelt had not been president and Germany had consolidated its power, the international system could have developed into a conflict-prone multipolarity. Perhaps if Truman had not been president and Stalin had made major gains in Europe and the Middle East, the Soviet empire would have been stronger and bipolarity might have persisted longer. Perhaps if Eisenhower or Bush had not been president and an alternative leader had been less successful in avoiding war, the American ascendency would have been driven off track (as it was for a time by Vietnam). Given its economic size and favorable geography, structural forces would likely have produced some form of American primacy by the end of the twentieth century. But leaders' decisions strongly affected the timing and type of primacy. In that sense, even when structure explains a lot, agency within structure makes a difference. Some see history as an overwhelming river whose current is shaped by the large structural forces of climate and topography. But there is a difference between portraying human agents as clinging to a log swept along by the current and protraying them as white-water rafters trying to steer and fend off rocks, occasionally overturning and sometimes succeeding,

So leadership matters, but how much? There will never be a definitive answer. Scholars who have tried to measure the effects of leadership in corporations or laboratory experiments have sometimes come up with numbers in the range of 10 or 15 percent depending on the context.[77] But these are structured situations where change is often more linear. In unstructured situations, such as postapartheid South Africa, the transformational leadership of Mandela rather than one of the alternative African leaders made a huge difference. American foreign policy is structured by institutions and a constitution, but external crises can cause a context much more susceptible to transformational leadership, for better or worse. Since foreign policy events are path dependent, relatively small choices by leaders, even in the range of 10 or 15 percent, can lead to major divergent outcomes over time. Moreover, in a period of crisis, choices may lead to radically divergent paths. As the counterfactual examples above suggest, some presidential decisions made a significant difference in the creation of American primacy. But incremental presidents like Eisenhower and Bush were as important as the transformational presidents. Transformational leadership is not necessarily better (in the sense of more effective) than incremental leadership in foreign policy, and an inspirational style is not necessarily better than a transactional one, but as Robert Frost put it, when two paths diverge in a wood, taking the one less traveled by can sometimes make all the difference.

Ethics and Good Foreign Policy Leadership

Leadership experts often argue that transformational leadership has a moral dimension. Unfortunately, they sometimes muddle their analysis by building their values into their definitions.[1] They are correct to draw our attention to values, but their claims for the moral superiority of transformational or inspirational leadership are not justified.

What is good foreign policy leadership? "Good" has two dimensions: effective and ethical. A good sword cuts well, but it can be used for aggression or defense. A good thief steals a lot of money, but we still condemn the means by which he or she gets it. Democratic electorates want their leaders to be effective fiduciaries in protecting and advancing national interests, but American exceptionalism and moralism mean the followers also judge their leaders in moral terms. That raises the issue of the relationship between success and moral judgments. We do not simply look back and pronounce leaders "good" if they have been successful.

In practice, we judge ethics in three dimensions: ends, means, and consequences. The term "ends" is sometimes ambiguous, referring to outcomes (as in "ends do not justify means") and goals or intentions (as in "her ends

TABLE 3.1. TWO MEANINGS OF GOOD LEADERSHIP

Good	Effective	Ethical
Goals	Balance of realism and risk in vision	Values of intentions and goals
Means	Efficiency of means to ends	Quality of means used
Consequences	Success in achieving group's goals	Good results for in-group and for outsiders

were just"). I want to focus on the latter. Effective ends or goals combine realism and risk in a vision that can be implemented, while ethical ends and goals are judged by the morality of the intentions and vision. Good goals have to meet our moral standards, as well as a feasibility test. Effective means are those which achieve the goals, but ethical means depend on the quality, not just the efficacy, of the approaches employed. As for consequences, a leader's effectiveness involves achieving the group's goals, but ethical consequences mean good results not just for the in-group but for outsiders as well. Of course in practice, effectiveness and ethics are often closely related. A leader who pursues unrealistic goals or uses ineffective means can produce terrible moral consequences for followers. For example, even if we attribute good intentions to George W. Bush's invasion of Iraq, unrealistic goals and inadequate means had immoral consequences. Thus inadequate contextual intelligence and reckless reality testing that produce bad consequences can become an ethical failure. Conversely, a leader's good intentions are not proof of what is sometimes misleadingly called "moral clarity."

Those who justify foreign policy actions simply because they are based on moral intentions or, conversely, simply because they are successful are practicing one-dimensional moral judgment. The quality of moral reasoning requires consideration and balancing of all three dimensions. For example, consider the Vietnam War. Some argued that it was a moral war because American goals were to protect free South Vietnamese from the evils of totalitarian communism, but this reasoning ignored the questionable means the United States used, and its reckless disregard for the foreseeable consequences and the reasonable prospects of success. The result was immoral consequences. Good moral reasoning must be three dimensional.

The quality of moral reasoning can be separated from the issue of relativity and ultimate proof. Some people believe that because moral judgments are ultimately relative, they are merely a matter of personal tastes, like whether one prefers vanilla or chocolate ice cream. David Brooks observes that many young people today make that mistake. "Rejecting blind deference to authority, many of the young people have gone off the deep end to the other extreme: 'I would do what I thought made me happy or how I felt. I have no other way of knowing what to do but how I internally feel.'"[2]

Even if ultimate metaphysically based judgments cannot be proven, however, it does not follow that all moral reasoning is equal. One can apply standards of logic, causation, and consistency to judge the quality of moral reasoning. For example, when a fundamentalist broadcaster argues that homosexuality is an abomination because Leviticus 18:22 says so, you can point out that Leviticus 25:44 also states that one may possess slaves provided they are purchased from neighboring nations. Does that mean it is all right for Americans to own Canadians but not Australians?[3] Or if someone says nuclear weapons are good because "God gave them to us to protect the free world," one can ask why God also gave them to North Korea rather than South Korea. We can apply reason to judge the quality of moral arguments even if we cannot produce definitive proof. And, of course, one can ask if moral reasoning is simplistic and one dimensional or not.

Ethical Standards for Judging Leaders

Some writers treat great leaders like forces of nature that stand above all ethical reasoning. Isaiah Berlin criticizes historians who treat Alexander, Caesar, Attila, Mohammed, Cromwell, or Hitler "like floods and earthquakes, sunsets, oceans, mountain: we may admire or fear them, welcome or curse them, but to denounce or extol their acts is as sensible as addressing sermons to a tree (as Frederick the Great pointed out)." But as Berlin notes, this amoral doctrine of historical inevitability is not scientific and ignores the "limited but nonetheless real area of human freedom."[4] We can and do judge leaders' ethical choices.

But should leaders be judged by the same moral standard as ordinary citizens? Take the biblical injunction that "thou shalt not kill." In choosing a roommate or spouse, that commandment would rank high on the list of desired moral values. At the same time, most people would not vote for an absolute pacifist to become president of their country. Presidents have a fiduciary obligation to protect the people who elected them, and under certain circumstances that may involve ordering troops into battle to kill people.

In their private capacity, leaders are held to common moral standards. In democracies, at least, their personal acts are punishable by law as well as by loss of followers' trust. A president who killed an aide could be impeached, tried, and jailed. On the other hand, the role of a public leader may require a president to overcome a private aversion to taking human life. Even in less dramatic circumstances, followers want leaders to protect and advance their interests even if it sometimes involves deception. Up to a point, they often want leaders to sacrifice their personal scruples and depart from everyday moral rules in order to advance the group interest. As for justice, experimenters have found that people "preferred in-group-favoring leaders over fair ones."[5]

The resulting dilemma for leaders sometimes creates a problem called "dirty hands." Because they have a fiduciary responsibility, leaders may have to do things they would not be willing to do in their private lives. As trustees they have an additional set of moral obligations.[6] Michael Walzer argues that if it is right for a leader to try to succeed, "then it must also be right to get one's hands dirty. But one's hands get dirty from doing what it is wrong to do."[7] Walzer uses the example of a leader who orders a man tortured to discover the location of a terrorist bomb in a city and prevent the loss of innocent life, even though he personally believes torture is wrong. In addition, there are sometimes two equally compelling and conflicting standards in the same public sphere, and the problem of dirty hands is unavoidable.

Max Weber famously distinguished an ethic of ultimate ends from an ethic of responsibility. In the former, absolute moral imperatives must not be violated for the sake of good consequences, but an ethic of responsibility must focus on the results. Weber warns that "he who seeks the salvation of the soul, his own soul and others, should not seek it along the avenue of politics."[8] In the philosophical traditions of the Western Enlightenment, ethicists distinguish a deontological or rule-based approach associated with Immanuel Kant from a consequentialist approach associated with utilitarians such as Jeremy Bentham and John Stuart Mill. The two traditions provide important strands of contemporary moral reasoning in the West today. One can try to reconcile the positions by including the importance of future rules and institutions as a key consequence that must be weighed. Nonetheless, though rule (or institutional) consequentialism can sometimes lead to the same decision as that advocated by the deontologist, it does not completely resolve the basic differences.

A third, less prominent, tradition is called "virtue ethics" and can be traced back to Aristotle and the ancient Greeks. It pays attention to the cultivation of virtuous traits of character rather than the following of deontological or consequentialist rules for decision. It emphasizes being more than doing; the worth of the agent more than the morality of the decision. Moral virtues are fixed dispositions to do what is morally commendable. Good character is no guarantee of good action, but when someone makes an immoral decision, we often say he or she is acting "out of character." A leader can do wrong without being a bad person. A good leader cultivates virtues and uses experience to develop judgment. "Ethical behavior should not be the outcome of careful and laborious calculation and reflection; it should be immediate, spontaneous, governed by intuition"; behavior that "arises from serious attention to the relevant facts, not in place of them."[9]

In terms of our categories of intention, means, and consequences, virtue ethics places particular emphasis on the first dimension, just as deontologists stress the second, and utilitarians the third. As one philosopher concluded, "It is not clear that one must accept only one of these approaches while rejecting the others. . . . Even though moral philosophy may often seem a very different enterprise in the hands of Mill, Kant and Aristotle—the one neglecting what the other takes to be of chief importance—we have noticed many common themes and even many shared conclusions among these writers."[10]

But the danger of virtue ethics and intuition is the absence of any larger standards for objective judgment. If leaders develop engrained moral habits like Aristotle's classical virtues of character—courage, justice, prudence, and temperance—the dangers of character-based intuitionism become less acute. But different cultures and groups shape character in different ways. Moral intuitions are not all the same. A virtuous character in some cultures would not seem so in another. Osama bin Laden developed a character and a religious sense of justice and courage that allowed him to commit what we see as mass murder, but it probably also allowed him to sleep soundly.

Take Harry Truman's decision to drop the atomic bomb on Hiroshima and Nagasaki in an effort to end World War II. He has said he did not lose sleep over the decision.[11] In a war where millions of lives had already been lost, Truman was told that he could save hundreds of thousands of lives by avoiding a land invasion of the Japanese home islands. Moreover, the numbers killed at Hiroshima (and at Nagasaki) were fewer than those who had been killed in the conventional fire-bombing of Tokyo or Dresden. The issue remains hotly contested, but the contemporary middle-ground judgment among historians is that the number of American lives potentially saved might have been under fifty thousand, and that while the Japanese emperor was not ready to surrender, the war might have ended before an invasion in November.[12]

Was Truman's act morally justified? Strict deontologists and just-war theorists would answer that two wrongs do not make a right, and that the deliberate destruction of so many innocent civilians can never be justified. Institutional consequentialsts might agree on the separate grounds that using the atomic bomb against civilians set a terrible precedent, but other consequentialists could reply that nuclear deterrence helped prevent World War III, and that Truman later redeemed himself by refusing to use nuclear weapons when General MacArthur urged him to do so in the Korean War. By the time of his farewell address in 1953, Truman declared that "starting an atomic war is totally unthinkable for rational men."[13] That taboo against nuclear use has lasted for seven decades.

If Truman had refused to drop the bomb because of his personal moral beliefs, at what price does a leader's concern about personal integrity translate into selfishness and a violation of followers' trust? Could Truman have met his moral obligations both to American soldiers and to Japanese civilians? Either way, he had to choose between rights and thus encounter the problem of dirty hands.[14] There are no easy answers to such problems, and recent scientific discoveries suggest that evolution may have hard wired the dilemma into the human brain.[15]

Kenneth Winston argues that in daily practice, people's sense of moral obligation tends to come from three sources: One is a sense of conscience, which is personally or religiously informed and leads individuals to try to achieve a sense of moral integrity. A second involves rules of common morality that society treats as obligations for all individuals, and a third is codes of professional ethics and conventional expectations that might be considered the duties of one's role.[16] Leaders are subject to all three, and these different sources of moral obligation are frequently in tension with each other. Often there is no single solution. As Isaiah Berlin also noted, since "the ends of men are many, and not all of them are in principle compatible with each other, then the possibility of conflict—and tragedy—can never wholly be eliminated from human life, either personal or social."[17]

Many societies have ethical systems that stress impartiality and have an analog to the golden rule—do unto others as you would have them do unto you. Your interests and my interests should be treated the same way. John Rawls used the wonderful metaphor of an imaginary veil of ignorance about our initial relative positions to illustrate justice as fairness. However, appealing to an intuitive sense of fairness—treating others as you would want to be treated, not playing favorites, and being sensible to individual needs—does not always provide a solution. Amartya Sen invites us to imagine a parent with a flute and three children, each of whom wants the flute.[18] The first child says,

"I made it"; the second says, "I am the only one who can play it"; and the third says, "I have no other toys." Even with a thought experiment about deciding behind a veil of ignorance in which none of the children knows which one is which, the principle of justice as fairness remains unclear in some cases. In such instances, the parent (or leader) may find it more appropriate to turn to a procedural or institutional solution in which the children bargain with each other or agree on a lottery or on a neutral figure to decide how time with the flute will be allocated or shared. The parent can also teach or coach the children about sharing, which is a different image of leadership, as persuasion and education rather than exercise of authority. Teaching followers about process and institutions—helping a group decide how to decide—is often one of the most important moral roles that leaders (and parents) play.

Self-Serving versus Group-Serving Deception

Sometimes leaders have different objectives from those of a large part of their group, and rather than reveal the differences, they deceive their followers. When such actions are self-serving, as in cases of corruption or narcissistic ego gratification, moral censure is easy. Sometimes leaders invest in educating the group to a different point of view. They transform their followers' moral choices, and we tend to praise their moral leadership. In some instances, however, leaders find it impossible to educate their followers adequately in time, or followers are too deeply divided to reach a consensus that will sustain group action. Indeed, as the political scientist George Edwards has pointed out (and as Franklin Roosevelt discovered in the 1930s) it is often very difficult for American presidents to change the views of the public.[19]

In such circumstances, some leaders may take a paternalist view and decide to deceive their followers for what they see as their followers' larger or later good. John F. Kennedy misled the public about the role of Turkish missiles in the deal that ended the Cuban Missile Crisis in 1962.[20] Franklin Roosevelt lied to the American public about a German attack on an American destroyer. As Winston Churchill once put it, particularly in wartime, the truth may be "so precious that she should always be attended by a bodyguard of lies."[21] The political scientist John Mearsheimer argues that given the low levels of trust in international relations, "international lying, in other words, is not necessarily misconduct."[22]

The fact that consequences may sometimes justify leaders' violation of norms about honest means does not signify that all lies are equal, or that we must suspend moral reasoning in such cases. Machiavellian deception is often part of a smart strategy, for example, in bargaining to get a deal or even in bringing a group to accept new goals. But intentions matter. Deception that is purely self-serving turns from a strategy that may benefit others into selfish manipulation of others. Even if one admits that deception may sometimes be necessary, one can still ask about the importance of the goal, the availability of alternative means to achieve that goal, whether the deception can be contained or is likely to spread through precedent or example, the damage done to various victims of the deception, and the accountability of the deceivers (whether it can be discovered and explained later).[23]

Eric Alterman argues that presidential lies "inevitably turn into monsters that strangle their creators."[24] The more leaders use deception on their followers, the more they erode trust, weaken institutions, and create damaging precedents.[25] For example, Roosevelt's lies about a German attack on the USS *Greer* might have been justified on the consequentialist grounds of the importance of awakening the American people to the threat from Hitler, but Alterman thinks it also set a precedent that Lyndon Johnson could later use to obtain the Tonkin Bay resolution that contributed to the escalation of the Vietnam War. Moreover, it is all too easy for leaders to think they are telling a noble lie for the good of their followers when they are merely lying for political or personal convenience. That makes it all the more important that we engage in moral reasoning about the nature of the trade-offs that leaders make between their ends and means.

Costs, Risks, and Luck

Even if we excuse a lie like Roosevelt's on the grounds that the consequences can sometimes justify the means, we can still make moral judgments about how leaders distribute the risks and costs of their actions. Rash assessments of reality that impose high risks on others can be condemned on moral as well as effectiveness grounds. People who try to climb mountains accept a degree of risk, but a team leader still has to make sure that the whole group understands the balance between risk and achievement. It is one thing to pose a grand vision that leads people up a mountain; it is another to lead them too close to the edge of a cliff.

How much risk should a leader take on behalf of his or her followers? Aristotelian ethics celebrates a golden mean of avoiding excess or deficiency, in effect a prudent approach to risk that suggests transactional more than transformational leadership. But prudence may lead to missed opportunities. In some circumstances, a people benefit from a leader making a big bet rather than a series of incremental bets. For example, after Munich, Roosevelt bet on war with Hitler, though he was tactically prudent and incremental in explaining his bet to the American public. And Truman made a big bet in establishing the Marshall Plan and NATO after 1947. In contrast, Eisenhower placed a series of smaller incremental bets that produced eight years of peace and prosperity during the height of the Cold War. Most of George H. W. Bush's bets were like Eisenhower's, with the exception of a big bet on German unification.

Machiavelli famously celebrated what he called a leader's "virtu" as a combination of imagination, boldness, shrewdness, and determination. He noted that leaders who are foxes cannot defend against wolves, but that those who act like lions are vulnerable to snares. Sometimes it is better that a leader be a lion; sometimes, a fox. The appropriate behavior depends on an accurate assessment of the circumstances—which is sometimes called "judgment" or, as I called it earlier, contextual intelligence. For Machiavelli, "Those who rely simply on the lion do not know what they are about. . . . He who has known best how to employ the fox has succeeded best."[26]

Finally, when assessing leaders' actions in terms of the risks and costs imposed on others, one must consider what the philosopher Bernard Williams called "moral luck." Williams points out that the painter Paul Gauguin deserted his French family to travel to Tahiti. The result was the creation of some of the world's finest art, and many see the consequences as justifying his mistreatment of his family. Yet if Gauguin's ship had sunk en route to Tahiti, he would be remembered primarily as a run-of-the-mill painter and a callous man who deserted his family. Williams argues that in our moral reasoning about such cases, it matters how intrinsic the cause of the failure is to the project itself. A shipwreck would be "too external to unjustify him, something which only his failure as a painter can do."[27] And even then one could distinguish failing as a painter because of indolence or because of inadequate talent. Had Gauguin reached Tahiti and failed as a painter, we would not justify his desertion of his family. The stroke that felled Woodrow Wilson in the midst of his campaign for ratification of the Versailles Treaty was like a shipwreck, but Wilson's stubborn refusal to permit compromise was to a political leader as failure to paint well would have been to Gauguin.

Some dimensions of luck are purely fortuitous. Machiavelli warned of the role of "fortuna," but people can also help to make their luck. Judging luck requires a baseline of what would be a reasonable estimate of the probability of success, how much risk to assume in the circumstances, and who will bear the costs of the risk. Jimmy Carter had bad luck when a helicopter collided with a plane during the attempt to rescue the hostages in Iran. He bore much of the political risk himself, and the military risk was born by professionals, but even so, he could be blamed for inadequate training or an overly complex plan. George W. Bush encountered bad luck in some of the aspects of his efforts at nation building and stabilization in Iraq, but some of that bad luck arose from his reckless reality testing and inadequate attention to details. Reckless reality testing and unnecessary risk taking may be part of "bad luck," and it is that dimension that deserves moral blame rather than the part that is "pure" chance.

Conversely, many sports teams practice and analyze their opponent's game so that they can capitalize on errors and benefit from "good luck." In football games, turnovers of possession of the ball start with one team's error, but the outcome depends on the preparations and skill of the other team. The contextual intelligence and prudent judgments of Eisenhower and George H. W. Bush contributed to the "lucky" avoidance of any nuclear incidents that would have disrupted the creation of the American era in the 1950s or at the end of the Cold War. Because we weigh consequences so heavily in our moral judgment of leaders, history tends to be kind to the lucky and unkind to the unlucky, but we can still judge them in terms of the means they used, the causes of their luck, and how they capitalized on that luck.

That still leaves open the question of when is the appropriate point at which to judge leaders. Failures at one point in history may look more successful at a later time. Wilson failed to bring his country into a League of Nations, but a quarter century later the United States joined the United Nations. George W. Bush liked to make comparisons to Harry Truman, who left office with low popularity because

of the stalemated Korean War but later recovered in public
esteem. Some historians doubt history will be as kind to
Bush because Truman's role in fostering European recovery and building the NATO alliance were seen as solid accomplishments at that time, whereas "Bush, by contrast,
lacks any success of comparable magnitude to compensate
for his mismanagement of the Iraq war."[28] Far from being
beleaguered by the war, however, Bush persevered because
of his "unconquerable faith in the rightness of his Big Idea"
that history is moving toward democracy. "I believe a gift
of that Almighty to all is freedom."[29] Whether the loftiness
of his vision and his analysis of the context led people up
the mountain or over a cliff may require a decade or more
to be fully clear. Truman's biographer David McCullough
suggests that "about 50 years has to go by before you can
appraise a presidency—the dust has to settle."[30] But this
is far too lax a standard to help us make judgments in the
here and now. For one thing, the more distant an outcome
is in time, the more other causes feed into the chain of causation and the more difficult to credit or blame an act by a
leader a half century earlier.

The other reason to focus on more contemporaneous
judgments is that it allows us to look at the processes that
leaders followed in terms of assessing the context and risks
as described above. One of the most important skills of
good leaders is to design and maintain systems and institutions. This relates both to effectiveness and to ethics.
Poorly designed institutions are those that fail to achieve
a group's purpose not in each particular instance, but over
the long term. Well-designed institutions include means for
self-correction as well as ways of constraining the failures

of leaders.[31] Poorly designed or led institutions can also lead people astray. Obedience to institutional authority can be bad at times. Several decades ago a famous experiment at Yale encouraged students to administer simulated brutal electrical shocks to their colleagues, and a simulated prison experiment at Stanford also demonstrated the capacity of intelligent people to submit to authority. The recent case of Abu Ghraib prison reminds us of both the importance and the danger of poorly designed institutions. The Abu Ghraib guards were reservists without special training who lacked supervision and were given the task of softening up detainees. It is not surprising that the result was various forms of torture.[32] The moral flaws were not simply in the prison guards, but also in the higher-level leaders who created and failed to monitor a flawed institutional framework.

Ethical leadership involves not merely inspiring people with a noble vision, but creating and maintaining the systems and institutions that allow effective and moral implementation. This is a test that Theodore Roosevelt failed in the Philippines. Ronald Reagan articulated inspiring visions while George H. W. Bush did not, but Reagan's inattention to institutions produced the Iran/Contra scandal while Bush's well-organized process avoided potential accidents during the dismantling of the Cold War. The good outcome depended on more than "dumb luck."

DUTIES BEYOND BORDERS

Not only are ethical standards for judging leaders more complicated than those we use for judging fellow citizens in daily life, but the context of foreign policy adds an additional level of complexity.[33] To what extent should leaders pay attention to the rights, institutions, and welfare of those who are not their fellow citizens? Skeptics argue that where there is no sense of community, there are no moral rights and duties, and that the classic statement about ethics in international politics was Thucydides' rendering of the Athenians' response to the Melians' plea for mercy: "The strong do what they will and the weak suffer what they must."

If international relations were simply the realm of "kill or be killed," then presumably there is no choice, and there would be no role for morality. Ought implies can. But international politics consists of more than mere survival, and pretending choices do not exist is merely a disguised form of choice. While it is weak, there is a degree of international human community. To think only in terms of narrow national interests is simply smuggling in values without admitting it. The French diplomat who once told me, "What is moral is whatever is good for France," was ducking hard choices about why only French interests should be considered. The leader who says "I had no choice" often did have a choice, albeit not a pleasant one.

Anarchy means "without government," but international anarchy does not necessarily mean chaos or total disorder. International affairs lack the discipline of a domestic leviathan, but there are rudimentary practices and institutions that provide enough order to allow some important choices: balance of power, international law and norms, and international organizations. These practices can provide help in the iterative games of prisoner's dilemma, and there is some evidence that international violence has been decreasing over time.[34]

Even in the extreme circumstances of war, law and morality sometimes play a role. The *just war doctrine* originated in the early Christian church as Augustine and others wrestled with the dilemma that if the good did not fight back, they would perish and only the bad would survive. It became secularized after the seventeenth century, and today it provides a broad normative structure that considers all three dimensions of good ends, discriminating proportional means, and the probability of successful consequences.[35]

Even more to the point for American foreign policy leaders is that their followers demand that they include moral considerations in foreign policy. Americans like to believe that their country and culture represent a higher moral standard than those of the old world from which they seceded. American exceptionalism is based both on liberal ideas and on the view that the American colonists had rejected the bad ways of a Europe they had left behind. That is one of the reasons that Woodrow Wilson's arguments for entering World War I had more appeal than the balance-of-power approach of Teddy Roosevelt.

Thus moral issues are inescapable for American foreign policy leaders. Their followers often demand some moral dimension. Nonetheless, different perceptions affect the way leaders frame their moral choices. To somewhat oversimplify, there are three main approaches to ethical questions in international relations. Realists see a world composed primarily of states that must turn to self-help to ensure their security in an anarchic world.[36] Order comes before justice, and prudence is a primary value. Liberals see a world composed of states and peoples with pooled and individual rights protected by norms, laws, and institutions. Cosmopolitans see a global society of individuals, each of equal worth, and whose interest and welfare should be treated equally regardless of artificial state borders.

These broad categories are not exclusive, and in practice leaders mix these views in sometimes inconsistent ways in the formulation of foreign policies. As a result there is no single view on what duties American leaders owe to foreigners, or when and what types of intervention are moral. Walter Mead identifies at least four major American traditions: one, stemming back to Andrew Jackson thinks in narrow and impatient national terms; a Hamiltonian tradition places more emphasis on national interest in the context of a balance of power; a Jeffersonian tradition stresses American moralism in a more unilateral context; and the Wilsonian tradition is more cosmopolitan.[37]

Attitudes toward sovereignty and intervention have changed over the past century, but the dilemmas of liberal interventionism have deep roots. When British Prime Minister Tony Blair defended liberal intervention in a speech in Chicago in 1999, one could hear echoes of debates between the liberal William Gladstone and the conservative Benjamin Disraeli in Victorian Britain. Reacting to Greece's war for independence, in 1821 John Quincy Adams issued his famous statement about not going abroad in search of monsters to destroy, but Americans entered the Spanish War in part goaded by Spanish human rights violations during a counterinsurgency campaign in Cuba. Teddy Roosevelt complained about Russian treatment of Jews and in 1904 proclaimed that "there are occasional crimes committed on so vast a scale and of such peculiar horror" that we should intervene by force of arms.[38] Woodrow Wilson intervened in Mexico because of concerns about democracy after the Mexican Revolution. An insular leader thinks only of the concerns of his or her own group, but a moral leader also considers the types and degree of consequences for those who are not members of the group. The image of a community of humankind may be a weak outer circle in a set of concentric circles of identity, but it still involves some degree of moral duties beyond borders. Failure to consider others is the moral failure of insularity.

The leadership theorist Barbara Kellerman accuses Bill Clinton of insular leadership in failing to respond to the genocide in Rwanda in 1994, and Clinton himself has criticized his reactions. Yet had Clinton tried to send American troops, he would have encountered stiff resistance in parts of his administration, the Congress, and public opinion. Particularly after the death of American soldiers in an earlier humanitarian intervention in Somalia, his followers were not ready for another intervention. Clinton has acknowledged that he could have done more to help the United Nations and other nations to save some of the lives that were lost in Rwanda, but good leaders today are often caught between their cosmopolitan inclinations and their more traditional obligations to the followers who elected them.[39]

Insularity is not an all-or-nothing moral dimension. In a world in which people are organized in national communities, a purely cosmopolitan ideal is unrealistic. For a leader to say there is an obligation to equalize incomes globally is not a credible obligation, but to say that more should be done to reduce poverty and disease can rally followers. As Kwame Anthony Appiah puts it, "Thou shalt not kill is a test you take pass-fail. Honor thy father and thy mother admits of gradations."[40] The same is true of cosmopolitanism versus insularity. We may admire leaders who make efforts to increase their followers' concern for the consequences of their actions on the out-group, but it does little good to hold them to an impossible standard whose pursuit could undercut their capacity to remain leaders.

Prudence and Criteria for Judgment

How then should we judge the ethics of presidents in foreign policy? They act not in an amoral world but clearly are acting in Max Weber's world of nonperfectionist ethics and peculiar anarchic context. Thus the realist norm of prudence is essential. Kenneth Winston argues that when judging leaders, we should remember that the abstract principles beloved of philosophers are not much help to practitioners, and that "the more rule-like the formulation, the more it fails to allow for the contingencies of effective action." Practical ethics requires a set of executive virtues and competences of which "prudence is the most central or paramount."[41] This is particularly true in international affairs, where the decisions of presidents and prime ministers can have such destructive effects. In the words of the great realist theorist Arnold Wolfers, the best one can hope for in judging the ethics of leaders in foreign policy is that they made "the best moral choices that circumstances permit."[42]

Such a broad rule of prudence is a good starting point, but it can easily be abused to justify almost anything short of nuclear war. What are some of the additional criteria we can use to reason about whether the presidents made "the best moral choices" under the circumstances? We can look at the quality of their consideration of all three dimensions of ends, means, and consequences. When we look at the ends or goals that presidents sought, we can expect a broadly moral vision, but we do not expect them to pursue justice similar to their domestic policies. After all, the great liberal theorist John Rawls believed that the conditions for his theory of justice applied only to a well-ordered domestic society. As Robert Jackson has argued, because of the diversity of human values around the world, "there can be no definitive answers about how to live in such a normative sphere. There can only be a general recognition of such diversity and respect for it."[43] Nonetheless, as Rawls argues, duties beyond borders for a liberal society should include mutual aid and respect for rights and institutions that ensure basic human rights while allowing people in a diverse world to determine their own affairs as much as possible.[44] Thus the criteria I suggest for judging prudent goals include a vision that expresses widely attractive values at home and abroad but also balances those values and assesses risks so that there is a reasonable prospect of their success. This means we judge presidents partly on their character and the moral quality of their intentions, but also on their contextual intelligence when it comes to assessing their ends and goals. A moral vision must be balanced by the realist dimension of prudence to have a reasonable prospect of success.

As for means that presidents use, when it comes to the use of force, we can borrow from the important and long-established norms of just-war theory. An ethical use of force must be proportional and discriminate. With respect to sovereignty and autonomy, I will use Rawls's liberal concern for minimal degrees of intervention in order to respect the rights and institutions of others. As for consequences, we can judge whether a president was a good trustee. Did he succeed in promoting American long-term interests (including an assessment of the role of moral luck as discussed earlier)? We can also ask whether he respected cosmopolitan values by avoiding extreme insularity. In pursuing American interests did he minimize the damage to others? And finally, we can ask the question raised by James McGregor Burns; did the president educate his followers to try to create and broaden moral standards at home and abroad. Table 3.2 presents a checklist that includes some of the criteria suggested by all three traditions of international normative theory: realism, liberalism, and cosmopolitanism.

Such a list is modest and by no means complete; nor does it provide a precise metric for comparisons. It does, however, draw on major ethical traditions to provide some basic guidance that goes beyond simple generalities about prudence as we look for answers case by case. As Winston argues, in applied ethics, "Cases are the mini-histories that, when carefully selected and effectively taught, help practitioners develop the competences they need to act effectively and well in public life."[45] So let's look at the cases of the eight men who presided over four phases of the creation of American primacy.

TABLE 3.2. SOME CRITERIA FOR JUDGING ETHICAL FOREIGN
POLICY LEADERSHIP

Ends/Goals	
Moral vision	Expresses broadly attractive values at home and abroad
Prudence	Balances values and risk
	Creates a reasonable prospect of success
Means	
Force	Use is proportional and discriminate
Liberal	Respects rights and institutions at home and abroad
Consequences	
Fiduciary	Good trustee for the long-term interests of Americans
Cosmopolitan	Minimizes damages to foreigners, not insular
Educational	Broadens followers' moral discourse at home and abroad

EIGHT PRESIDENTIAL CASES

Theodore Roosevelt

Roosevelt considered himself a "practical idealist." He once said, "I hold the man worthless who is not a dreamer, who does not see visions; but I also hold him worthless unless in practical fashion he endeavors to shape his action so that these dreams and visions can be partially realized." As a young man from a patrician family, there was nothing he wanted more "than to live up to his father's expectations of ethical behavior and personal duty."[46] As one biographer argues, "He was perhaps the most intense moralist to serve in the White House, and he supported a wide variety of reforms aimed at how people lived their lives."[47] In domestic politics he was a visionary and inspirational leader who pioneered an era of significant progressive reform. While he imbibed the ubiquitous racism of American life at the time, he could sometimes rise above it, as when he invited the African American Booker T. Washington to the White House, much to the chagrin of some southern supporters.

In international affairs Teddy Roosevelt was a strong believer in the superiority and civilizing mission of the Anglo-Saxons in general and the United States in particular. He was a balance-of-power realist who believed in the use of force, but he coupled that with an exceptionalist's idealism about the values the United States could bring to the rest of the world. "Roosevelt's emphasis on international security was not an exercise in cool Bismarckian calculation: instead it was intimately connected to his idealism. . . . Thus in foreign relations, Roosevelt believed that 'our chief usefulness to humanity rests on our combining power with high purpose.' "[48] At the same time, he believed that "life is strife," and he scorned those who were "servile in their dread of war."[49] He was irritated by what he saw as the unrealistic idealism of Woodrow Wilson.

In 1896 Roosevelt had complained about President Cleveland's failure to annex Hawaii because it meant the islands would be settled not by "white Americans, but of low caste laborers from the yellow races." He also believed that wars of conquest "may be fraught either with evil or with good for mankind, according to the comparative worth of the conquering and conquered people."[50] But Roosevelt was not alone in such insular views. While there were American anti-imperialists (like Mark Twain) with opposite views, social Darwinism and imperialism were the powerful ideas of the time. We can legitimately criticize Roosevelt and his contemporaries by today's prevailing standards, but it is more useful to assess them by the moral standards of their time. In that sense Roosevelt was better than some of his contemporaries. He did not let racism prevent him from working closely with some Asians. He admired Japan's efforts to modernize, and he even tried to work out solutions to anti-Japanese prejudice in access to education by Japanese immigrants in California. But he also had serious flaws even by the standards of his own day.

William Tilchin argues that "Roosevelt stands tall, far surpassing 'reasonable expectations' both in the way he deployed American power and influence and in the ethical component of his diplomacy. TR's foreign policy demonstrates the entire 'constellation of political virtues'—prudence, judgment, vision, good faith, courage, and others."[51] But this judgment is too gentle. Roosevelt is well remembered for the mediation of the Russo-Japanese War that produced a Nobel Prize, the Panama Canal, the Roosevelt Corollary to the Monroe Doctrine, the Great White Fleet, and improved relations with Britain and Canada among other accomplishments, but the record is more mixed than Tilchin implies if we look at some of the means that Roosevelt used.

In at least two significant instances, Roosevelt acted unethically even by the standards of his own time. In the case of the Philippines, where the American army killed and tortured large numbers of prisoners in an effort to suppress the insurrection, he encouraged a tough approach by General Adna Chafee (a friend whom he had fought alongside

in Cuba). "He did not want to hear bad news about atrocities, and dismissed the attacks by Twain, [Senator] Hoar
and other goo-goos as serving the enemy." He retaliated
against General Miles, the army chief of staff, who tried to
punish officers guilty of atrocities, and after the war ended
Roosevelt promoted Generals Young, Chafee, and Bell,
three of the most ruthless commanders, to the top position
of army chief of staff, "an indication of what the president, even on reflection, really thought about the harsh-
ness of the U.S. Army's conduct." As Ambassador Warren
Zimmerman concludes, "Roosevelt and Root tolerated the
atrocities, finding a scapegoat here and there but essentially
explaining away and covering up. It was a black mark on
Roosevelt's young presidency."[52] These events happened
early in his presidency and reflected the bellicose attitude
he had recently taken in the Spanish War, but even in 1906
he defended the Jolo massacre, in which his friend Brigadier
General Leonard Wood exterminated six hundred Moro
rebels, as "a brilliant feat of arms."[53] As contemporary
Senate hearings made clear, such actions violated American
law as well as being unethical. Nor could they be said to be
justified by the necessity of war, such as Truman's bombing
of Hiroshima. And while Roosevelt argued that such acts
were not official policy, he could not plead ignorance of the
problem as George W. Bush did about remarkably similar
incidents in Iraq a century later.

   The other instance of unethical behavior, though less
egregious and clear cut, was Roosevelt's encouragement
of the secession of Panama from Colombia in preparation for the building of a canal. The Panama episode also
involved aggressive and corrupt lobbying by a variety of

actors in Washington; a genuine secessionist sentiment in Panama; and inept politics in Colombia. Nonetheless, as Roosevelt boasted in 1908, "It could not have been accomplished save by me or by some man of my temperament." But there were ethical costs. "The arrogant dismissal of the constitutional practices of Colombia, the cynical rewriting of international law to fit U.S. policy, the unacknowledged role of the U.S. Navy, and the punitive treaty imposed on the fledging republic of Panama: None of these actions comported with Roosevelt's pious rationalizations." At a cabinet meeting shortly after the events, Roosevelt justified his behavior and asked Elihu Root if he had answered the charges against him. Root replied, "You certainly have Mr. President. You have shown that you were accused of seduction and you have conclusively proved that you were guilty of rape."[54] The building of the Panama Canal was an important step forward for American power, allowing the navy to sail in two oceans without a distant journey around Tierra del Fuego. Moreover, Roosevelt was abetted by Colombian incompetence. But some isthmus canal would have been built in Panama or Nicaragua sooner or later, and it might well have been accomplished without the questionable means that Roosevelt used.

A third ethical charge against Roosevelt is that he sold out the independent Kingdom of Korea to appease Japan and protect the Philippines. Certainly that fits with his realist views, and his actions in 1905 and 1908 encouraged Japan. It is far from clear, however, that Roosevelt's actions were crucial to the loss of Korean independence, because Japanese colonization was likely with or without American acquiescence. Nonetheless, Roosevelt's attitude toward the rights and institutions of the Korean kingdom, while consistent with imperialist attitudes of the time, were callous when judged by contemporary American rhetoric about rights, and not fully disclosed to the public at the time.

Whatever one thinks of Roosevelt's questionable means, his overall goals and vision for American foreign policy were consistent with a realist view of the world in which American power was increasing. He did a good job of balancing risk and prudence, advancing America as a power in global issues without taking any undue risks. For example, while mistrustful of both Russia and Germany, he was careful not to alienate either country in the aftermath of his mediations at Portsmouth or Algeciras. His goals were less insular than those of his predecessors as president, and they modestly broadened the prevailing public views of the national interest. As for consequences, he successfully advanced American national interests, and, with the important exceptions noted above, without great harm imposed on outsiders.

But it would be hard to argue that Roosevelt raised or broadened moral standards at home or abroad. It is also difficult to see that he did much to educate his followers, the American public, about foreign policy. Defenders object to criticisms that Roosevelt failed to educate the public. Tilchin argues that "TR did his best to educate without undermining his various diplomatic endeavors, and he operated according to a constitutionally legitimate, if controversial, theory of presidential authority. His record as a statesman would have been extraordinary even had he enjoyed a more congenial political climate. Without that

climate, it was all the more extraordinary."[55] But evidence
of his failure is that his immediate successors did not follow Roosevelt's policies, and, as Henry Kissinger noted
eight decades later, there was less trace of Roosevelt than
Wilson in American foreign policy attitudes.

As I argued in chapter 2, Theodore Roosevelt was a
giant of a man (though only 5 feet 8 inches tall) and well
justified for his place on Mount Rushmore by his domestic
achievements alone. But despite his flamboyance, he was
not transformational in the creation of the American era,
and his flawed means could not be justified by their larger
consequences. Thus whatever the virtues and failures of his
ethical positions in foreign policy, they may have contributed something to the timing, but not to the creation, of the
American era. Sooner or later the Philippines insurrection
would have been put down, and sooner or later a canal
would have been built across the isthmus (though not necessarily in Panama). Unethical means were not a necessity.

THEODORE ROOSEVELT'S ETHICAL SCORECARD

Ends/Goals

Moral vision: expressed broadly attractive values	mixed
Prudence: balanced values and risk	good

Means

Force: used proportionally and discriminately	poor
Liberal: respected rights and institutions	mixed

Consequences

Fiduciary: was good for American interests	good
Cosmopolitan: minimized damage to others	poor
Educational: broadened moral discourse at home and abroad	poor

William Howard Taft

Taft was a moderate progressive conservative, a practicing member of the Cincinnati Unitarian Church and devoted to the principles of the law. He has been described as "an outstanding public servant, ruthlessly honest, aristocratically disdainful of political humbug, and incapable of hypocritically flattering the American public or catering to their baser whims."[56] He lacked the jugular political instincts of his predecessor, and he often ignored the partisan political costs of his decisions at his peril. He shared the generally prevalent optimistic view of American purposes and favored a significant American presence in the world, particularly through commerce and finance. He had expressed reservations about imperialism and the annexation of the Philippines but was a relatively just and impartial governor-general of the islands, and he was popular with large segments of the population. He took seriously the task of preparing the Philippines for eventual independence. He was a conscientious and careful cabinet member, loyal to President Roosevelt.

Unlike his predecessor, Taft did not articulate a unique vision of American foreign policy and imparted little that was new to the American public. In that sense he presided over but contributed little to the first phase of the creation of American primacy. He focused mostly on the traditional domains within the scope of the Monroe Doctrine and ensured the smooth construction of the Panama Canal. His preferred diplomatic methods were financial and economic influence, but he was prepared to use force for relatively modest interventions in Central America and the

Caribbean. In the case of Mexico, however, he was careful not to become militarily involved. Taft was a strong believer in law and arbitration as a means of ensuring world peace, but the treaties he negotiated with Britain and France were only modest steps in such a direction. After his presidency, he became a strong supporter of a league of nations. Taft was a decent and conscientious man who was sandwiched between two giants of the first phase of the creation of the American era, but he left little mark of his own on American foreign policy.

TAFT'S ETHICAL SCORECARD

Ends/Goals

Moral vision: expressed broadly attractive values	poor to mixed
Prudence: balanced values and risk	good

Means

Force: used proportionally and discriminately	good
Liberal: respected rights and institutions	mixed

Consequences

Fiduciary: was good for American interests	mixed
Cosmopolitan: minimized damage to others	mixed
Educational: broadened moral discourse at home and abroad	poor

Woodrow Wilson

Like Roosevelt and most American leaders early in the twentieth century, Wilson also considered himself an idealist. But in his words, he was "an idealist with the heart of a poet." Wilson sought inspiration from "a long view of human nature derived more from literature than from empirical data." Son of a Calvinist minister, "inheritance and indoctrination made Wilson a Presbyterian; temperament made him an especially devout one—a Presbyterian priest." These traits meant that he found occasion "to interpret as the Lord's will convictions other men attributed to less remote sources, occasion to hallow and moralize issues that other men considered secular and casual."[57] And Wilson could be notably stubborn about compromise on issues he regarded as moral once his mind was made up. In the view of Alexander and Juliette George, Wilson's self-esteem was damaged during his strict upbringing, and "to compromise meant to yield to interference in that sphere of authority in which he sought compensatory gratification."[58] Whatever the merits of this interpretation of the origins of his stubbornness, one should not exaggerate the impact of such stubbornness on Wilson's effectiveness as a politician under normal circumstances. In the words of John Milton Cooper, he was "one of the most careful, hardheaded, and sophisticated idealists of his time."[59]

Like Teddy Roosevelt, Wilson shared the racial prejudices as well as the prevailing Anglo-Saxon chauvinism of his times. He did not hesitate to intervene in Mexico and the Caribbean. On the other hand, while Roosevelt justified his policies with a realist analysis, Wilson's vision of the international system had liberal and communitarian elements. These liberal views were not original with Wilson, but he gathered and synthesized them into what he considered a more moral American approach to foreign policy. He did not coin the term "self-determination for peoples," but he adopted it without fully confronting all the implications of that ambiguous principle, and it was applied at

Versailles in a very imperfect fashion. Wilson first used the term in speech in February 1918, and a year a half later he confessed, "When I gave utterance to those words, I said them without a knowledge that nationalities existed, which are coming to us day after day. . . . You do not know and cannot appreciate the anxieties that I have experienced as the result of many millions of people having their hopes raised by what I have said."[60]

Wilson understood the balance of power, but he believed that a league of nations based on a collective security alliance against aggressors would be more peaceful and just than the cynical alliances required to balance power. And contrary to many caricatures, Wilson did not launch a crusade for democracy. In his 1917 war message to Congress, he was careful to use the passive construction: "the world must be made safe for democracy." A year later he told journalists, "There isn't any one kind of government which we have the right to impose upon any nation. So that I am not fighting for democracy except for those people that want democracy."[61]

How then should we judge Wilson's goals and vision? Were they really as impractical as critics have portrayed them? Arthur Link has made a case for what he calls "the higher realism of Woodrow Wilson." He argues that the so-called realists at Versailles lived in "a dream, a nightmare, of unreality" that produced the flawed settlement that laid the basis for World War II. In contrast, Wilson sought a peace without victory, mistrusted the use of force for material gain, and saw America's mission not as material aggrandizement but as leading nations into a new international community organized to achieve right ends.

"Over and over he argued that this was the only kind of peace that would prove acceptable to the American people in the short run and to the moral opinion of the world in the long run, in short, the only kind of settlement that could endure." Link notes that the American realist George Kennan revised his views of Wilson in 1991. At that point Kennan concluded that "in his vision of the future needs of world society, I now see Wilson as ahead of any other statesman of his time.[62]

But Link's and Kennan's revised assessments raise an interesting question about ethical foreign policy leadership. If a leader diagnoses a problem correctly in the long term but not the short term, or if the leader lacks the requisite leadership skills to implement the diagnosis, the result is a leadership failure. Link may be correct that Clemenceau and Orlando's classical European realist vision contributed to a flawed treaty that set the scene for German revanchism, but the tragedy of the 1930s was that sensible policy fell between the two stools of the balance of power and collective security visions. Both Clemenceau and Wilson share some of the blame for the 1930s debacle that Link blames solely on Wilson's opponents. Perhaps if Wilson had possessed the leadership skill to ensure American participation in the League, this outcome might have been forestalled, but his lack of emotional intelligence and his mismanagement of the process at Versailles and later in the bargaining with the Senate contributed to the failure. Wilson's limited contextual intelligence about international affairs meant that he was not sufficiently alert to the pitfalls that awaited him. Despite his noble vision, his failure as an *effective* leader led to unintended but foreseeable consequences that contributed to his failure as an *ethical* leader. And sadly, the situation was made worse by the bad moral luck of his untimely stroke.

Where Wilson succeeded ethically was not as a foreign policy leader, but as a thought leader. In 1919 when he was idolized, and again decades later, he became a symbol of a new type of international relations. His influence was global and long term, and his calls for self-determination helped to stimulate demands by colonized peoples who were given short shrift by the leaders at Versailles. As the historian Erez Manela observed, "Rhetoric in international affairs has unintended audiences, and actions beget unintended consequences. . . . The Wilsonian moment marked the beginning of the end of the imperial order in international affairs."[63]

Wilson's ideas for an international organization were not implemented by his countrymen for more than two decades, and then only in part. Nonetheless, Wilson strongly affected his successors, particularly Franklin Roosevelt and Harry Truman. As Henry Kissinger has noted, even Richard Nixon was influenced by Wilson. The historian John Morton Blum sums it up well: "Wilson's triumph was as a teacher, his lesson written in the copybooks of generations unborn when he taught."[64] In this dimension, Wilson exceeded Teddy Roosevelt. But there is a difference between leadership in ideas and leadership in policy. Wilson had a less insular vision than Roosevelt, but less contextual intelligence in shaping a prudent balance between values and risk. Wilson's means were more respectful of the rights of others than were Roosevelt's, and in terms of long-term consequences he did more to raise and broaden moral

standards, but in the decade that followed their administrations of American foreign policy, Roosevelt proved to
be the more successful fiduciary in achieving the goals of
his followers.

WILSON'S ETHICAL SCORECARD

End/Goals

Moral vision: expressed broadly attractive values	good
Prudence: balanced values and risk	poor

Means

Force: used proportionally and discriminately	good
Liberal: respected rights and institutions	good

Consequences

Fiduciary: was good for American interests	poor
Cosmopolitan: minimized damage to others	mixed
Educational: broadened moral discourse at home and abroad	mixed

Franklin Roosevelt

Franklin Roosevelt believed in God and an American mission, but he wore his religion and his ethics much more
lightly than did Woodrow Wilson. Moreover, Roosevelt
was very much a man of compromise, often changing positions, and leaving followers and observers to wonder what
he really believed. He was notorious for keeping subordinates in the dark, and he referred to his leadership skills
as that of a juggler trying to keep many balls in the air at
once. He often seemed to follow rather than lead public
opinion.

Roosevelt's leadership relied heavily on deception.
Gary Wills argues that "what polio did was make him

preternaturally aware of others' perceptions of *him*. This increased his determination to control those perceptions. People were made uncomfortable by his discomfort. He needed to distract them, direct their attention to subjects he preferred; keep them amused, impressed, entertained. That meant he had to perfect a deceptive ease, a casual aplomb, in the midst of acute distress. He became a consummate actor." He used devices like the pince-nez, cigarette holder, and careful stage management to distract attention from his disabled lower body. "This regime of deception reached its climax in the 1944 campaign, when the terminally ill Roosevelt tried to show his strength in an open-car ride through New York City, where he was pelted by driving rain."[65]

Roosevelt always remained close to public opinion and never let himself get too far ahead of it. I noted earlier that this accounts for why he used an inspirational style in domestic affairs, where the public supported his transformational reform objectives, yet used a transactional style in foreign policy, where he hid his transformational goals from an isolationist public. Some have seen this timidity as a moral failing. For example, he could have saved many more Jews from Hitler's Europe if he had braved anti-Semitic reactions in the American public and loosened immigration restrictions before the war. And at the beginning of the war, a similar attitude led to the violation of the human rights of Japanese American citizens. Even regarding his major objective of preparing the public to enter the war on the side of the Allies, he quickly retreated when many of his trial balloons were shot down.

At the same time, he would try to engineer what seemed to be independent crises and incidents that would educate public opinion in the direction he wished to move. But what is the line between trying to educate the public and manipulating the public? What degree of deception is permissible in a democracy? Earlier I argued that one bright line is between self-serving and group-serving deception. Roosevelt was not above, and sometimes enjoyed, occasional self-serving lies, but most of his major deceptions were for what he thought was the good of the public he was deceiving. A reasonable test is how an impartial observer who shared his goals might judge the action, and how damaging the actions are to trust and institutions. At one end of the spectrum might be deceptions where a leader does not disclose his or her true objectives but that is typical of all politicians; at the other end of the spectrum would be a systematic series of outright lies that could cause loss of confidence in institutions. It was one thing to campaign in 1940 on a promise of no war (after all the moralistic Wilson did the same in 1916), or to use misleading labels like "destroyers for bases" or "lend lease" as disguises for military aid programs. It was quite different to deliberately tell the American public that the USS *Greer* had been attacked by a German submarine when it was the *Greer* itself that launched the attack.

Cathal Nolan has excused these lies on the consequentialist grounds that "in extremis it is sometimes necessary to violate the letter of the law in order to save the rule of law." Hitler posed such an existential threat that Roosevelt had no alternative but to deceive the public (though as we saw earlier, Bruce Russett has raised questions about the argument that he had no alternative). "Lying is a requisite of diplomacy, but the best diplomats and national leaders nonetheless lie only rarely and in extreme cases" because they know it destroys trust. On the other hand, Nolan is critical of Roosevelt's use of lies to support his wartime and postwar plans. He "deliberately deceived the American public about the internal character of the Soviet Union, a maneuver that proved quite harmful in the end." As Robert Dallek has noted, Roosevelt knew full well there was no freedom in the Soviet Union. In Nolan's view, "the appropriate criticism thus is not that Roosevelt lied. The real problem was that he may have lied *unnecessarily* before he tried an all-out campaign of using the presidential bully pulpit to convince anti-Soviet Americans that massive material aid to Russia was in the direct and vital interest of the United States."[66] And one of the effects of the deception is that Americans were less well prepared for dealing with the Soviet Union at the end of the war.

In terms of his goals and vision, Roosevelt maintained a reasonable balance between risk and realism in his foreign policy, though he did not express it clearly to the public, and he was less clear in Asia (where his contextual intelligence was lower) than in Europe. But his ethical goals were limited by a degree of insularity, and a bolder position could have saved more Jews and done less damage to the rights of Japanese Americans. His domestic means were constitutional, but the degree of deception he used may have been damaging for institutions in the long term. At the same time, his plans for a postwar United Nations and associated economic institutions and his pressure for decolonization showed a liberal concern for rights. But it is in the consequences that Roosevelt's foreign policy had the largest ethical importance. His choice to see Hitler as a threat and to prepare America for entry into World War II rather than to accept the isolationist trend of public opinion was a major moral decision with enormous implications for the creation of the American era. Yes, he had the moral luck of the Japanese attack and Hitler's declaration of war, but he had prepared to capitalize on that luck. After Pearl Harbor, he began a process of educating the public for a sustainable role in the world, though ironically not adequately about the Soviet Union. And he failed to educate his poorly prepared understudy who would succeed him when the great actor's health failed.

ROOSEVELT'S ETHICAL SCORE CARD

Ends/Goals

Moral vision: expressed broadly attractive values	good
Prudence: balanced values and risks	good

Means

Force: used proportionally and discriminately	mixed
Liberal: respected rights and institutions	mixed

Consequences

Fiduciary: was good for American interests	good
Cosmopolitan: minimized damages to others	mixed
Educational: broadened moral discourse at home and abroad	good

Harry Truman

Harry Truman, the accidental president who built on Roosevelt's transformation, could not have been a more different type of leader from his predecessor. In the words of one biographer, "He possessed little or no charisma, struggled with an ego more fragile than most observers have

understood, and had extreme distaste for the need to manipulate others. He was, however, a good manager and, on
the important things, a person of sound judgment, not least
because he understood his weaknesses. Often dismissed by
contemporaries as a 'little man' because his deficiencies
were more apparent than his strengths, he actually was one
of the more important and successful of twentieth-century
presidents."[67] Another biographer comments that "this so-
called little man from Missouri surrounded himself with
people who were better educated, taller, handsomer, more
cultivated, and accustomed to high-powered company, but
that didn't bother him. He knew who he was."[68] This apparent contradiction suggests that there were different lay-
ers of Truman's self-confidence. Just below the surface was
the sensitivity and insecurity that led him to write intem-
perate letters to critics, but below that was a sense of self
that led him to stuff the letters into a desk drawer rather
than send them, and eventually to have the courage to fire a
disruptive military hero like Douglas MacArthur. Truman
had good emotional IQ, and that is important because his
contextual IQ about international affairs was limited. Unlike Roosevelt, he had to rely on delegation and institution-
alizing foreign policy.

In terms of vision and goals, as we mentioned in the
last chapter, Truman came into office committed to implementing Roosevelt's grand design. But he also had a strong
moral vision of his own. "He was a Wilsonian idealist who
deeply believed in American international leadership; the
duty of American foreign policy was to promote the bet-
terment of mankind. He could speak with great eloquence
of TVAs [Tennessee Valley Authorities] for remote parts of

the world and of the progress yet to come in human affairs. He probably would have been at a loss in any attempt
to discuss totalitarianism on a theoretical basis. But . . .
he understood its challenge, whether Nazi or Soviet, better than did many of his contemporaries."[69] Truman was
a man who expressed the proverbial basic values of the
American Midwest.

Truman did a reasonable job of prudently balancing risk
and realism in his goals. He was quite cautious in the early
days after the war, and he developed his transformational
objectives only after on-the-job learning from experience
and in consultation with skilled advisors. His management
of the Berlin Airlift in response to Soviet efforts to squeeze
American troops out of the old German capital was a
model of prudence. In Korea, he acted incautiously given
Acheson's earlier exclusion of the peninsula from America's defense perimeter and given the poor preparation of
American troops. Truman wanted to implement Wilson's
vision of collective security as embodied in the UN Charter.
In that sense, his vision was liberal and international rather
than nationally insular, but a realist might have been more
cautious about the risks involved.

In terms of means, there was little deceptive about Truman. His methods were honest, constitutional, and trustworthy. He respected and built institutions at home and
abroad and was attentive to questions of autonomy and
rights. Where he has been faulted on means is on the questions of the indiscriminate killing of civilians through the use
of nuclear weapons to end the war in Japan. As discussed
earlier, it would have taken a bold move by Truman to stop
their use, and he saw no reason to do so. The principles of

discrimination and proportionality had already been massively violated by the firebombings of Dresden and Tokyo, among others, and the public was eager to end a war that Japan had started. In that sense the train had already left the station by the time Truman became president, and he went along with the consensus. But on the question of nuclear use against North Korea and China five years later, he deserves great credit. By refusing to treat nuclear weapons as normal, even at the price of accepting a politically difficult stalemate in Korea, Truman helped to return to the practice of limited war and to institutionalize a nuclear taboo.

As for the consequences, Truman's decision to keep an American presence overseas and to build strong alliance institutions was crucial to the establishment of the American era. Except in the eyes of residual isolationists, he was a good fiduciary in advancing American long-term interests. Moreover, he did so with attention to the needs of outsiders and programs to assist them, such as the Marshall Plan and technical assistance. Both the Marshall Plan and his support for the United Nations can be seen as raising and broadening moral standards. And while Truman was no great orator, he and his cabinet tried to educate the American people to the importance of maintaining American leadership in the reconstruction and stabilization of the postwar world. Some critics have faulted Truman for changing George Kennan's doctrine of containment to an overly universal doctrine of defending free peoples everywhere that eventually set the scene for the Vietnam War, but it is difficult to blame Truman for Vietnam, and without his universalism the strategy would have been more difficult to sell to the American people. Moreover, by infusing values into a realist strategy, he set the framework for the institutionalization of the Atlantic alliance. It is true that Harry Truman indulged in American moralism, but it is also true that he had a largely ethical foreign policy that made a major contribution to the creation of American primacy.

TRUMAN'S ETHICAL SCORECARD

Ends/Goals

Moral vision: expressed broadly attractive values	good
Prudence: balanced values and risks	good

Means

Force: used proportionally and discriminately	mixed
Liberal: respected rights and institutions	good

Consequences

Fiduciary: was good for American interests	good
Cosmopolitan: minimized damage to others	mixed
Educational: broadened moral discourse at home and abroad	good

Dwight Eisenhower

According to one biographer, Dwight Eisenhower's leadership was "firm, fair, objective, dignified, he was everything most Americans wanted in a President." If there was one word to describe reactions to him, it was "trustworthy."[70] He understood soft power and how to draw people to him. Richard Nixon once said that when it came to decision making, Dwight Eisenhower was "the most unemotional and analytical man in the world," but Fred Greenstein argues that what was striking about Ike's leadership was "not his lack of passion, but the freedom of his public actions from extraneous emotion."[71] Eisenhower was well endowed with emotional intelligence. He also had strong moral convictions. He was a free-market Republican, a staunch anticommunist, and committed to America's role in the world even when many in his party wanted to turn back the clock.

At the same time, Eisenhower lacked transformational objectives and was no moral crusader. In 1952, when he accepted the Republican nomination, he called for the party to join him in a crusade to clean up Washington, but critics later "found it difficult to discover what his crusade was aiming at. There was no stirring call to arms, no great moral crusade, no idealistic pursuit of some overriding national goal." As Ambrose argues, in 1953 Eisenhower had wanted "to provide moral leadership that would both draw on and illuminate America's spiritual superiority to the Soviet Union, indeed to all the world." But on the great moral issues of the day that affected American soft power—civil rights and McCarthyism—he failed to speak out. And on the Third World, which he hoped to line up with the Western democracies, "failure was caused by Eisenhower's anti-Communism coupled with his penchant for seeing Communists wherever a social reform movement or a struggle for national liberation was under way. His overthrow of popularly elected governments in Iran and Guatemala, his hostility toward Nasser, his refusal to seek any form of accommodation with Castro, his extreme overreaction to events in the Congo, were one result. Another was a profound mistrust of the United States in the Third World. A third result was an over-commitment in Indochina, based on an obsession with falling dominoes."[72]

Eisenhower came into office with more knowledge of international affairs than any president before or after him.

That produced superb contextual intelligence about the limits of American power and the importance of prudence in managing crises. And managing crises was what he did best, whether it be Korea in 1953, Dien Bien Phu in 1954, Quemoy and Matsu in 1955, Hungary and Suez in 1956, Sputnik in 1957, Berlin in 1959, or the U-2 spy plane in 1960. "Eisenhower managed each one without overreacting, without going to war, without increasing defense spending, without frightening people half out of their wits. He downplayed each one, insisted that a solution could be found, and then found one. It was a magnificent performance."[73] Moreover, he made important institutional improvements in the National Security Council process that helped to maintain an orderly foreign policy.

In ethical terms, Eisenhower's vision and goals were modest and balanced, but his record on means was more mixed. The covert actions that overthrew the popular regimes of Arbenz in Guatemala and Mossadegh in Iran violated local autonomy, and Eisenhower by his own admission "realized full well that United States intervention in Central America and Caribbean affairs had greatly injured our standing in all of Latin America."[74] Nonetheless, in the context of a bipolar Cold War, he felt it essential to forestall any possible communist advances. But one can question whether these leftist nationalist regimes would have led to communist states, and the long-term memories and repercussions in both countries were unfavorable to the United States. The consequences were not good for the United States or the local peoples over the long term.

On a different aspect of means related to the use of force, however, Eisenhower deserves a great deal of moral praise.

He resolutely opposed numerous recommendations for the use of nuclear weapons in the Korean, Dien Bien Phu, and Quemoy-Matsu crises. As he told one advisor, "You boys must be crazy. We can't use those awful things against Asians for the second time in less than ten years."[75] At one point in 1954, Eisenhower turned to Admiral Radford, chairman of the Joint Chiefs of Staff, and said, "Suppose it would be possible to destroy Russia. I want you to carry this question home with you: gain such a victory, and what do you do with it? Here would be a great area from the Elbe to Vladivostok . . . torn up and destroyed, without government, without its communications, just an area of starvation and disaster. I ask you what would the civilized world do about it? I repeat that there is no victory except through our imaginations."[76] In many instances Eisenhower argued from the point of view of prudence, but this indicates that he went beyond insular American interests and included a cosmopolitan element in his moral reasoning about nuclear weapons.

Eisenhower's refusal to use nuclear weapons did not prevent him from threatening to use them for the sake of deterrence and compellence. He used the nuclear threat to help bring an end to the Korean War, and he increased American reliance of nuclear deterrence as a means of cutting back on the expense of conventional forces. At the same time, he tried to advance arms-control agreements with the Soviets. By the very nature of his deterrent bluff, however, Eisenhower could never level with the American people about his real view on nuclear weapons. As he once replied to his press secretary's warning against too much clarity on the issue of nuclear weapons at a press conference, "Don't worry Jim. If that question comes up, I'll just confuse them."[77]

Ike's nuclear policy was consistent with his general style of governing described earlier. He posed publicly as a benign monarch above the fray, while carefully controlling like a prime minister behind the scenes. As Greenstein points out, "He was no Machiavellian; he recognized the importance of honesty and intellectual clarity in private deliberations but took it as an unspoken axiom that public language was to be adapted to the circumstances at hand and toward the best possible consequences."[78] Such an approach to deception is far down the scale from the deception practiced on the public by Franklin Roosevelt, but such means limited Eisenhower's ability to educate the public. In general, Eisenhower's foreign policy leadership produced good consequences for Americans and others by prudent avoidance and management of crises. Although he lacked transformational goals, eight years of peace and prosperity are pretty impressive consequences.

EISENHOWER'S ETHICAL SCORECARD

Ends/Goals

Moral vision: expressed broadly attractive values	good
Prudence: balanced values and risks	good

Means

Force: used proportionally and discriminately	good
Liberal: respected rights and institutions of others	mixed

Consequences

Fiduciary: was good for American interests	good
Cosmopolitan: minimized damage to others	mixed
Educational: broadened moral discourse at home and abroad	mixed

Ronald Reagan

Ronald Reagan is often cited as an example of a moral foreign policy leader par excellence. A movement conservative, he is remembered for speeches that issued a strong call for moral clarity—at Westminster in 1982 where he predicted that the spread of freedom would "leave Marxism-Leninism on the ash heap of history"; in Florida in 1983 when he called the Soviet Union "an evil empire"; and in Berlin in 1987 where he demanded, "Mr. Gorbachev, tear down this wall." His appeal rested on "knowing that mere reason, essential though it is, is only half of the business of reaching momentous decisions. You also need solid-based instincts, feelings, whatever the word is for the other part of the mind. 'I have a gut feeling,' Reagan said over and over again, when he was working out what to do and say." Reagan believed "there are simple answers to many of our problems—simple but hard. It's the complicated answer that's easy because it avoids facing the hard moral issues."

Yet Reagan was not as simple as he made himself out to be. He was a popular man but preferred his own company; a champion of small towns who lived in big cities; an exponent of family values who divorced his first wife and had distant relations with his children. He was "a true believer who lacked the usual personality defects of the type: a sectarian with an ecumenical style."[79] Like Franklin Roosevelt, Reagan lacked a first-class intellect but made up for it with a first-class temperament. He radiated optimism and illustrated the point that style can influence substance. As David Gergen observes, Reagan changed how we think

about ourselves. While he could be "so dreamy and inattentive to detail that he allowed dramatic mistakes to
occur," Gergen considered him the best leader since Franklin Roosevelt.[80]

When people today call for a "Reaganite foreign policy,"
they tend to mean the moral clarity that went with Reagan's
simplification of complex issues and his effective rhetoric
in the presentation of values. Not only is this inadequate
moral reasoning for reasons explained earlier, but it also
mistakes the success of Reagan's moral leadership, which
included the ability to bargain and compromise as he pur-
sued his policy. For example, when asked at the 1988 Moscow summit whether he still considered the Soviet Union
to be an evil empire, he replied that "I was talking about
another time, another era."[81]

Nonetheless, clear and clearly stated objectives can educate and motivate the public. The key question is whether
Reagan was prudent in balancing aspirations and risks
in his goals and objectives. As we saw in the last chapter,
Reagan's transformational objective was to revise the status quo of the Cold War, and in addition to diminish or
abolish nuclear weapons. He contributed to the first, but
less to the second. Some people have argued that his initial
rhetoric in his first term created a dangerous degree of tension and distrust in US-Soviet relations that increased the
danger of a miscalculation or accident leading to war, but it
also created incentives to bargain that Reagan put to good
advantage when Gorbachev came to power in Reagan's
second term. As for insularity, Reagan expressed his values
in universal terms, though he was sometimes accused of
hypocrisy for focusing on Soviet violations of human rights

while ignoring the violations perpetrated by a number of American Third World client regimes. He was quite prepared to live with apartheid in South Africa and support regimes that used death squads in Central America, and it took two years after the first protests before he reduced his support for the Marcos regime in the Philippines.

With regard to means, Reagan had a mixed record. The circumvention of legal means during the Iran/Contra issue set a bad precedent in terms of domestic as well as international norms and institutions. And the Reagan Doctrine of using covert action to fight wars against leftist regimes in Central America not only raised legal issues with Congress but also included the mining of harbors in Nicaragua, a country with which the United States was officially at peace. Whether these transgressions of autonomy and institutional restraints were justified by realist necessity is disputable, but the damage was real.

In terms of consequences, Reagan undoubtedly advanced the national interests of the United States, though, as we saw earlier, most of the credit for ending the Cold War and the Soviet Union belongs to Gorbachev. In any event, Reagan took good advantage of the opportunity in a manner that was not limited just to insular American interests. On other issues, such a placing Marines in Lebanon and then withdrawing them when they were attacked, or bargaining for the return of hostages, some analysts argue that he set bad precedents for dealing with terrorism that had unfortunate long-term consequences. Reagan's moralistic rhetoric broadened moral discourse at home and abroad, but its educational effect was sometimes subverted by actions (such as support for apartheid in South Africa) that appeared hypocritical in terms of the values that Reagan proclaimed for himself and for his country. By and large, Reagan had an ethical foreign policy in the goals he set, and most of the larger consequences to which he contributed, but not always in terms of the means he used.

REAGAN'S ETHICAL SCORECARD

Ends/Goals

Moral vision: expressed broadly attractive values	good
Prudence: balanced values and risks	mixed

Means

Force: used proportionally and discriminately	mixed
Liberal: respected rights and institutions	mixed

Consequences

Fiduciary: was good for American interests	good
Cosmopolitan: minimized damage to others	mixed
Educational: broadened moral discourse at home and abroad	good

George H. W. Bush

George Bush's family background and his experience as a navy fighter pilot in World War II left him with a strong sense of civic responsibility.[82] His long career in various government positions ranging from Congress to UN ambassador to director of the Central Intelligence Agency equipped him with the best contextual intelligence about international affairs since Eisenhower. As one former foreign service officer who served under Bush argued, "Bush's accomplishments in ending the Cold War, unifying Germany, amassing the Gulf War coalition that defeated Saddam Hussein in that same year, and in then pivoting to start Israeli-Palestinian negotiations at Madrid make him arguably the most successful foreign policy presidents of the last 50 years."[83] Or as Bush himself summed it up (with Brent Scowcroft), "What Harry Truman's containment policy and succeeding administrations had cultivated, we were able to bring to final fruition. Did we see what was coming when we entered office? No, we did not, nor could we have planned it. . . . The long-run framework of Bush foreign policy was very deliberate: encouraging, guiding, and managing change without provoking backlash and crackdown. In the short run, the practical effort included as well a certain amount of seat of the pants planning and diplomacy. . . . We eluded the shadow of another Versailles."[84]

As his own account describes, Bush did not have transformational objectives, with one exception: the unification of Germany. On this important issue he resisted the advice of Margaret Thatcher, Scowcroft, and others, apparently out of a sense of fairness and responsiveness to his friend Helmut Kohl's efforts to unify the country. After a visit with Kohl in 1983, Bush had concluded that "Germany was a solid democracy that had done penance for its sins and that 'at some point you should let a guy up.' "[85] In October 1989, even before the opening of the Berlin Wall, Bush responded to a call from Kohl by publicly stating that "I don't share the concern that some European countries have about a reunified Germany." At the same time, he was careful to let Kohl and others take the lead. When the Berlin Wall was opened, partly by an East German mistake, on November 9, Bush was criticized for his low-key response. But he had made a deliberate choice not to humiliate the Soviets or gloat: "I won't beat on my chest and dance on the wall" was his response—a model of emotional intelligence in a leader. Such self-restraint helped to set the stage for the successful Malta summit a month later.[86]

Bush was concerned about avoiding disaster in a world that was changing dramatically. As he and his team responded to the forces that were largely outside of his control, he set goals and objectives that balanced opportunities and realism in a prudent manner. For example, some critics have faulted him for not being more forthcoming in supporting the national aspiration of Soviet republics like Ukraine in 1990, or for failing to go all the way to Baghdad to unseat Saddam Hussein in the Gulf War, or for sending Scowcroft to Beijing to maintain relations with China after the Tiananmen massacre of 1989, but in each instance Bush was limiting his short-run objectives in order to pursue long-term stability as a goal. As we saw earlier, other critics have complained that Bush did not set more transformational objectives in relation to Russian democracy, or the Middle East, or nuclear nonproliferation at a time when world politics seemed fluid, but again he remained focused on questions of stability more than new visions. In ethical terms, although Bush did not express a strong moral vision, it is difficult to make the case that he should have been less prudent and taken more risks.

As for means, Bush was respectful of institutions and norms at home and abroad, going to Congress for authorization of the Gulf War, and to the United Nations for a resolution under chapter 7 of the charter. Although a realist in his thinking, he could be Wilsonian in his tactics. In terms of proportionate and discriminate use of force, his termination of the ground war in Iraq after only four days was motivated in part by humanitarian reactions to the slaughter of Iraqi troops as well as the concern that Iraq not be so weakened that it could not balance the threatening power of its neighbor Iran. While his invasion of Panama to capture (and later try) Manuel Noriega may have violated Panamanian sovereignty, it had a degree of de facto legitimacy given Noriega's notorious behavior. And when Bush organized his coalition to prosecute the Gulf War, he not only worked with the United Nations but included a number of Arab countries who were not needed for military purposes but for the legitimacy that they added to the coalition. With his careful combination of hard and soft power, Bush established a policy that raised moral standards at home and abroad and was capable of being sustainable in the future.

In terms of consequences, Bush was a worthy fiduciary in accomplishing American goals and managed to do so in a manner that was not unduly insular and with minimal damage to the interests of foreigners. He was careful not to humiliate Gorbachev, and to manage the transition to Yeltsin in Russia. At the same time, not all foreigners were adequately protected, for example, when Bush assigned a lower priority to Kurds and Shia in Iraq, to dissidents in China, or to Bosnians who were embroiled in a civil war in the former Yugoslavia. In that sense, his realism set limits to his cosmopolitanism. Ironically, one of his final acts, sending American Marines to Somalia to save starving civilians, was a violation of his realism and in the end turned out badly for his successor.

Could Bush have done more under the circumstances? Possibly, or perhaps he might have done more in a second term, and losing that opportunity was an instance of bad moral luck. And with a better set of communications skills, Bush might have been able to do more to educate the American public about the changing nature of world they faced after the Cold War. But given the uncertainties of history, I am inclined to agree with the former career diplomat Nicholas Burns that Bush had one of best foreign policies of the past century in both the effective and ethical meaning of the term.[87]

Bush's Ethical Scorecard

Ends/Goals

Moral vision: expressed broadly attractive values   mixed
Prudence: balanced values and risks   good

Means

Force: used proportionally and discriminately   good
Liberal: respected rights and institutions   good

Consequences

Fiduciary: was good for American interests   good
Cosmopolitan: minimized damage to others   good
Education: broadened moral discourse at home   mixed
    and abroad

Good Foreign Policy

As we saw earlier, contrary to the assumptions of leadership theory, there is no evidence to conclude that leaders with transformational objectives or inspirational styles were better in the sense of more effective in the creation of American primacy. The same conclusion holds for "better" in its ethical meaning. While the judgments rendered above are rough summaries of complex phenomena that have many aspects, they are a good enough first approximations to falsify claims for the moral superiority of the transformational or inspirational foreign policy leaders among the eight men who presided over the creation of the American era. The best record goes to the incremental and transactional George H. W. Bush, and poorest records belong to the transformational and inspirational leaders Theodore Roosevelt and Woodrow Wilson. In sum, the creators of the American era had good goals, but some used questionable means. They all believed in the exceptionalism of the United States and the good that American values could bring to the rest of the world. They often were reacting to external challenges and threats, but they also believed that American primacy was a good thing.

Was the creation of primacy good for Americans? Certainly, it helped to secure American values of life, liberty, and the pursuit of happiness, but it involved economic and political costs as well as benefits. Power is not good or bad per se. It is like calories in a diet: more is not always better. Too much power can be a curse rather than a benefit if it distorts priorities and leads to overconfidence and inappropriate strategies. Lord Acton famously warned that "power corrupts and absolute power corrupts absolutely," and states can suffer from a "power curse."[88]

In opposing America's costly and counterproductive involvement in the Vietnam War, Senator J. William Fulbright warned against what he called "the arrogance of power." Perhaps the great increase of American power after World War II led to the strategies that contributed to defeat in Vietnam and the 1970s retrenchment two decades later.

But Acton's dictum is not an iron law. Kennedy and John-son may have fallen into a trap, but Eisenhower had even more power resources than they, and yet he chose a more prudent path (which Kennedy criticized). As we have seen, leadership choices matter. While arrogance and hubris are problems for all humans, particularly powerful ones, many of the leaders who presided over the development of American primacy (such as Franklin Roosevelt, Truman, Eisenhower, Reagan, and Bush) were responding more to perceived external security problems than to an imperial urge to dominate. Sometimes these threats produced risks to life and liberty at home, but the political system also had a self-righting resilience.[89] The historical record shows that hubris is a risk, but it is not inevitable.

Whether American primacy has been good or bad for the world is a different and important question, though not the subject of this book. Obviously, the answer depends on who was affected, and how, and what were the realistic alternatives. One would expect different answers in North and South Korea, in North and South Sudan, and from various elites and insurgents. Some scholars argue that the creation of the American era involved interventions that deprived citizens in places like Central America or Iran of their autonomous development. And support for repressive regimes that were part of the containment of Soviet com-munism led to widespread violations of human rights.[90]

If one believes, however, that international politics is not yet (or ever) ready for world government or even a Wilso-nian solution to anarchy, then global public goods such as security and welfare will depend on the actions of the most powerful states. Many scholars have pointed out that one thing worse than American leadership is no leadership at all.[91] Order does not produce justice, but some degree of order is often a precondition for it. Complete anarchy can produce highly immoral consequences.

Some scholars, such as Samuel Huntington and John Ikenberry, have gone a step further and argued that whatever the excesses of American primacy, the fact that the world's largest country had a liberal economy and polity had important implications not only for the creation of an open international economic system but also for the spread of democratic values and human rights.[92] In that sense, American exceptionalism mattered. The largest country plays a disproportionate role not only in the provision of global public goods but also in the transnational promotion of values. It matters that the United States was an open society, or what Ikenberry labeled a "liberal hegemon." A German or Soviet victory in the twentieth century would have produced a very different world. American primacy allowed degrees of freedom of choice to others and an openness that was not always true of past hegemonies, and it presents opportunities for institutional change as presidents adjust foreign policy to the dramatic shifts in the context of power in this century. We turn to that question in the next chapter.

CHAPTER 4

Twenty-First-Century Leadership

The twentieth century ended with an extraordinary imbalance in world power resources. The United States was the only country able to project military force globally; it produced more than a quarter of the world product; and it had the world's leading soft power resources in its universities and entertainment industry. Because the United States represented nearly half of world military expenditure and was formally allied to Europe and Japan, the remaining countries could not create a classical balance to American power. Moreover, the change from the Soviet Union to Russia reduced the nuclear threat that had helped to deter some American actions during the Cold War. American primacy seemed well established abroad and at home.

DID LEADERS MATTER?

To what extent did presidential leadership matter in creating this extraordinary situation? In chapter 2 we looked at the roles of the eight twentieth-century leaders who presided over the four positive phases in the creation of American primacy and asked what difference their leadership contributed beyond what could be predicted by structural explanations. In addition, we asked whether

those leaders who are sometimes called "transformational" from the point of view of their transformational
objectives and inspirational styles made greater contributions than those who were primarily incremental in their
objectives and transactional in their styles. After examin-
ing plausible counterfactuals, I concluded that all except
Teddy Roosevelt and Taft made contributions (though
not always as intended) beyond what could be explained
simply by structural forces, and that while two presidents
with transformational objectives (Franklin Roosevelt and
Truman) made particularly important contributions to the
creation of the era of American primacy, two who had incremental objectives and a transactional style (Eisenhower
and Bush) may have been equally important by prudent
management that allowed favorable structural change to
occur and avoided potentially disastrous disruptions. I argued that a good analysis of leaders' roles in causation has
to look at the dogs that did not bark as well as those that
did. In chapter 3 I asked whether these eight men were
good foreign policy leaders in the sense of ethics as well as
effectiveness. Leadership theorists often assign a positive
normative value to transformational leaders, but I found
no evidence to justify such a preference after looking at
these presidents. The best ethical record belonged to the
incremental and transactional George H. W. Bush, and the
poorest records to the transformational and inspirational
Teddy Roosevelt and Woodrow Wilson.

In short, to answer the question posed in the first chapter: yes, leadership mattered in the creation of American
primacy. If the causes were purely structural, the process should have been much smoother. After all, America

represented roughly a quarter of world product both at the beginning and at the end of the century. World War I strengthened American power. A change in the structure of power resources cannot explain the interwar phase of retraction. A good explanation must take the (unwise) leadership decisions into account.

In the middle of the century, America came to represent nearly half of world product and held a monopoly on nuclear weapons. Over the next two decades, this share reverted to the century-long norm. That decline was structural, but it was accompanied by unwise leadership decisions related to the Vietnam War that created a second period of retraction. But America's return to its earlier share of world product did not lead to Nixon's expected multipolarity and the end of American primacy. On the contrary, American primacy increased in the 1980s and 1990s as the distribution of power shifted from bipolar to unipolar. As we saw, a major cause of this shift was long-term economic structural change that weakened the Soviet Union. But again leadership mattered, most importantly in Gorbachev's unintended acceleration of the demise of the Soviet Union, but also in the successful choices made by Reagan and Bush that allowed the United States to capitalize successfully on the structural changes.

So leadership matters, but not exactly in the ways that leadership theorists predict. Their expectation that transformational leaders make all the difference and incremental/transactional leaders are simply routine managers greatly oversimplifies the role of leadership. Appeals for transformational leadership are not necessarily the best way to understand the leadership needs of American foreign policy in the twenty-first century. Ironically, the first president of this century began with a domestic focus and an incremental foreign policy but became transformational; the second campaigned as a transformational leader but became largely incremental in his first term.

TRANSFORMATIONAL LEADERSHIP IN THE TWENTY-FIRST CENTURY

Foreign policy played almost no role in the 2000 election, but the crisis of September 11, 2001, produced a transformational foreign policy. A nonstate actor's attack on the homeland killed more Americans than did the Japanese government's attack at Pearl Harbor and had a profound effect on President Bush, his followers, and American public opinion. In 2001 George W. Bush started as a limited realist with little interest in foreign policy but became transformational in his objectives after the crisis. Like Wilson, Franklin Roosevelt, and Truman, Bush 43 turned to the rhetoric of democracy to rally his followers in a time of crisis.

Bill Clinton, the beneficiary of the primacy that was consolidated under the first President Bush, had also talked about enlarging human rights and democracy, but the 1990s was a period in which the American people sought normality and a peace dividend from the end of the Cold War rather than dramatic change. Clinton took a number of important steps in opening trade, creating fiscal stability, and bringing Russia and China into the global economy while simultaneously reassuring allies in Japan and Europe. After initial stumbles related to UN peacekeeping in Bosnia and

Rwanda, he used force in a number of humanitarian interventions. But in the view of historian John Lewis Gaddis, Clinton lacked a grand strategy and "allowed an illusion of safety to produce a laissez-faire foreign and national security policy."[1] Similarly, Zbigniew Brzezinski faulted Clinton for failing to develop a new strategy to take advantage of the opportunities opened by unipolarity.[2]

In contrast, Bush's 2002 National Security Strategy, which came to be called the Bush Doctrine, proclaimed that the United States would "identify and eliminate terrorists wherever they are, together with the regimes that sustain them." Preemption was a third element: America would not wait to act until after it was attacked. A fourth component of the doctrine was what Bush called his "freedom agenda."[3] The solution to the roots of the terrorist problem was to spread democracy everywhere. In an outburst of enthusiasm at the time, Gaddis called it "'Fukuyama plus force,' and designed to make terrorism as obsolete as slavery or piracy. . . . Iraq was the most feasible place to strike the next blow."[4]

This is not the place to rehearse the problems of the Iraq War. Bush invaded Iraq ostensibly to change the regime and to remove Saddam Hussein's capacity to use weapons of mass destruction. While he did not do enough to question the intelligence or manage the process, he cannot be blamed for the intelligence failure that attributed such weapons to Saddam since such estimates were widely shared by many other countries. While no weapons were found, American forces quickly overthrew Saddam. But the removal of Saddam did not accomplish the mission, and inadequate understanding of the context plus poor planning and management undercut Bush's transformational objectives. While some Bush administration defenders try to trace the causes of the 2011 Arab revolutions to American policies in Iraq, such arguments oversimplify causation and are denied by many of the primary Arab participants.

At home the Democrats were able to use Bush's foreign policy problems to win elections in 2006 and 2008 that repudiated his policies. Barack Obama won the presidency on a promise of withdrawal from Iraq, a more modest approach to regime change, and the view expressed in his inaugural address that "our power grows through its prudent use." While it is still too early for a definitive historical judgment on the Iraq War, what is clear at this point is that the twenty-first century opened with a crisis that led to failed transformational leadership.[5] The leader lost his followers.

It is interesting to compare Bush with the transformational leaders of the twentieth century that we have examined. George W. Bush is described as obsessed by the idea of being a transformational president; not a status quo operator like Bill Clinton. Secretary of State Condoleezza Rice praised the virtues of "transformational diplomacy," and veterans of the first Bush presidency like Brent Scowcroft observed that in 2003 the main divisions in foreign policy were not between liberals and conservatives, but between traditionalists and transformationalists.[6] Despite their shared genes, the policy of George W. Bush could not have been more different from that of his father. Members of the younger Bush's administration often compared him to Ronald Reagan or Harry Truman, but the twentieth-century president he most resembled was Woodrow Wilson.

There are uncanny similarities between Wilson and
George W. Bush. Both were highly religious and moralistic
men who were elected with less than a majority of the popular vote and initially focused on domestic issues without
any vision of foreign policy. Both were initially successful
with their transformational domestic agendas in the Congress. Both tended to portray the world in black and white
rather than shades of gray. Both projected self-confidence,
responded to a crisis with a bold vision, and stuck to it.
As Secretary of State Robert Lansing described Wilson in
1917, "Even established facts were ignored if they did not
fit this intuitive sense, this semi-divine power to select the
right."[7] And Secretary of State Colin Powell described Bush
as knowing "what he wants to do, and what he wants to
hear is how to get it done."[8] Contrary to popular political
calumny, Bush did not lack intelligence, but he rarely ex-
plored beyond his area of comfort. As British Prime Minister Tony Blair observed, "George Bush was straightforward
and direct. And very smart. . . . George had great intuition.
But his intuition was less . . . about politics and more about
what he thought was right and wrong. This wasn't stated
analytically or intellectually. It was just stated."[9]

Though Wilson started as an idealist and Bush as a realist, both wound up stressing the promotion of democracy
and freedom in the rest of the world as their transformative vision. And both defined visions that had a large gap
between expressed ideals and national capacities. Many of
Bush's speeches, particularly his second inaugural address
about a freedom agenda, sounded like Wilson could have
uttered them. Both Wilson and Bush tried to educate the

public to accept their transformational visions. But as political scientist Hugh Heclo argues, "Successful teaching requires ongoing learning on the teacher's part."[10] Similarly, Barbara Farnham distinguishes long-term education programs to extend the range of acceptability of policies from "selling efforts" that involve manipulation of preferences in the short run.[11] Bush's impatience hindered both his own learning and his ability as a teacher. In the words of a journalist who spent many hours with him, "He has a transformational temperament. He likes to shake things up. That was the key to going into Iraq."[12] In his own words, he was not interested in playing "small ball."[13] That impatient temperament also contributed to the organizational process Bush put in place that discouraged learning.

Wilson succeeded initially in educating a majority of the American people about his League of Nations, but he failed because he refused to make compromises with the Senate. Similarly, George W. Bush was initially able to persuade the American people of his proposed transformation of American strategy, and he was reelected in 2004, but he lost support (and the Congress) by 2006. The comparison illustrates that the prospects for transformational leadership in foreign policy are greatest in the context of a crisis. But even then, success requires a combination of soft power skills to attract people at home and abroad with a feasible vision, and hard organizational and political skills to implement the vision. Franklin Roosevelt and Harry Truman had the combination. Woodrow Wilson did not. Similarly, George W. Bush articulated transformational objectives but did not develop a successful strategy to accomplish them.

The Obama Presidency

This century's second president, Barack Obama, also expressed transformational objectives and came to power at a time of crisis. By late 2008 both the American and the world economy were in the midst of the worst financial crisis since the Great Depression. Indeed, some of Obama's economic advisors counseled him that unless urgent steps were taken to stimulate the economy, there was a significant chance of entering a full-scale depression. While he also inherited two ongoing wars, nuclear proliferation threats from Iran and North Korea, and the continuing problem of Al Qaeda's terrorism, Obama's early months in office were absorbed with dealing with the economic crisis both at home and abroad.

In contrast to Bush, the crisis that Obama faced was economic rather than security related, but Obama's temperament was different as well. While Obama had expounded a transformational vision in his campaign, his crisis responses were those of a pragmatist. Temperamentally, he was noted for his coolness in analysis under pressure, a term sometimes summed up by the phrase "no drama Obama." For example, his reaction to success in the highly risky cross-border raid that killed Bin Laden in 2011 but could have destroyed his presidency "was self-contained to the extreme: 'we got him,' was all he said."[14] Political scientist George Edwards criticizes Obama as a man who presented himself as a "transformational leader who would fundamentally change the policy and politics of America" and then overreached by thinking his ability to communicate and educate the public could change more than he could.[15]

But this criticism is more telling in regard to Obama's domestic program than in regard to his foreign policy.

Obama's rhetoric both in the 2008 campaign and during the first months of his presidency was both inspirational in style and transformational in objective. As several experts describe the campaign, "This image of a new domestic agenda, a new global architecture, and a transformed world was crucial to his ultimate success as a candidate."[16] Of course, campaign rhetoric always sounds more transformational as challengers criticize the incumbents, but Obama continued the transformational rhetoric with a series of speeches in the first year of his presidency, including his inaugural address; a speech at Prague proclaiming the goal of a nuclear-free world; a speech in Cairo promising a new approach to the Muslim world; and his Nobel Peace Prize speech promising to "bend history in the direction of justice." In part this series of speeches was tactical. Obama needed to meet his promise to set a new direction in foreign policy while simultaneously managing to juggle the legacy of issues left to him by Bush, any of which, if dropped, could cause a crisis for his presidency. Nonetheless, there is no reason to believe that Obama was being disingenuous about his objectives.

Obama had an "activist vision of his role in history," intending to "refurbish America's image abroad, especially in the Muslim world; end its involvement in two wars; offer an outstretched hand to Iran; reset relations with Russia as a step toward ridding the world of nuclear weapons; develop significant cooperation with China on both regional and global issues; and make peace in the Middle East."[17] His record of achievement on these issues in his first term was mixed. "Seemingly intractable circumstances turned him from the would-be architect of a new global order into a leader focused more on repairing relationships and reacting to crises—most notably global economic crisis."[18]

It is too early for a definitive judgment on Obama's foreign policy, and it played a relatively small role in the 2012 campaign. The *Economist* called the first term "a mixed bag," but the columnist David Brooks praised it as "flexible, incremental, and well adapted to the specific circumstances of this moment. Following a foreign policy hedgehog, Obama's been a pretty effective fox."[19] Some of the half-empty glasses were the results of intractable events; some were the product of early administration naiveté, such as the initial approaches to Israel, China, and Afghanistan. But Obama was quick to recover from mistakes in a pragmatic way. In the words of James Fallows, his main trait was to be adaptable to new realities rather than a prisoner of his transformational ideas.[20] Fareed Zakaria praised Obama's "strategic restraint."[21]

Although Obama did not disavow his rhetorical expressions of transformational goals regarding such issues as climate change or nuclear weapons, in practice his pragmatism was more reminiscent of incremental leaders such as Eisenhower and the first Bush. Despite his relative inexperience in international affairs compared to them, Obama showed a similar skill in reacting to a complex set of foreign policy challenges. This was demonstrated by his appointments of experienced advisors, management of a careful White House–centered process, and, above all, keen contextual intelligence, honed in part by having an African father, an anthropologist mother, and a childhood spent partly in Asia. At the same time, more of his life was spent in American elite institutions and involvement in domestic politics.[22] Obama's contextual intelligence about the world without much career experience remains something of an anomaly compared to Bush 41 or Eisenhower.

This is not to say that Obama had no transformational effects in his first term. He changed the course of an unpopular foreign policy; shifted from labor-intensive counterinsurgency to less costly uses of military and cyber power; increased American soft power in many parts of the world; and began a rebalancing of attention on Asia, the fastest growing part of the world economy. David Sanger detected what he called an "Obama Doctrine" (though he faulted the president for not communicating it more clearly): a lighter military footprint combined with a willingness to use force unilaterally when American security interests are directly involved; a reliance on coalitions to deal with global problems that do not directly threaten American security; and "a rebalancing away from the quagmires in the Middle East toward the continent of greatest promise in the future—Asia."[23]

The contrast between the killing of Bin Laden and the intervention in Libya illustrates the Obama Doctrine. In the former case, Obama personally managed a unilateral use of force. In the latter case, he demonstrated smart power by waiting until an Arab League and UN resolution provided the legitimacy that ensured that the soft power narrative would not be that of another American attack on a Muslim country. Then he shared the leadership of the hard power operation with NATO allies. An incautious comment by a midlevel White House official characterized the Libya policy as "leading from behind," and this became a target for political criticism, but as we saw earlier, Eisenhower was a great exemplar of knowing that sometimes it is most effective to keep a low profile and to lead from behind.

Indyk, Lieberthal, and O'Hanlon summarize Obama as "a competent pragmatist" who has "protected American interests well given the circumstances, . . . but he has not yet put his indelible stamp on foreign affairs or bent the arc of human history in the positive transformational way to which he aspires."[24] The merits of Obama's first-term shift from a transformational to an incremental approach are debated. Some critics argue that he was too cautious to take advantage of the revolutionary times, particularly in the Middle East. He made a big bet on a surge in Afghanistan (which may or may not pay off) and another on violating Pakistani sovereignty to kill Bin Laden (which worked), but most of his strategic choices have been cautious and hedged. There has been nothing akin to the Truman Doctrine and the Marshall Plan or George H. W. Bush's backing of German unification.[25]

Big bets, however, often involve big risks, and as we saw in the previous chapter that they raise important questions of what risks and costs foreign policy leaders should impose on their followers. Such bets should at least meet the just-war criterion of having a reasonable prospect of success, but even that is hard to judge. One of history's great strategists, Otto von Bismarck, successfully bet in 1870 that a manufactured war with France would lead to Prussian unification of Germany, but he also bet that he could annex Alsace-Lorraine, with enormous costs that became clear only later in 1914. Wilson made a costly and mistaken bet on the Versailles Treaty. Kennedy and Johnson made mistaken bets that Vietnam was a game of dominoes, not checkers, where Eisenhower, who coined the domino terminology, refused to intervene. And Nixon, who bet successfully on an opening to China, made a nearly simultaneous but mistaken bet on the destruction of the Bretton Woods monetary system. Franklin Roosevelt and Truman made positive transformational bets before and after World War II, but only after initial cautious approaches.

As we saw earlier, there is little evidence to support the general assumptions of leadership theory and public discourse that transformational foreign policy leaders are better in either ethics or effectiveness. For one thing, the concept of transformational leadership is too ambiguously defined to be useful unless it is more carefully specified. But even with objectives distinguished from style, the evidence does not support the view that leaders with transformational objectives or inspirational style are better. Other leadership skills outlined in the first chapter are more important than the usual distinction between transformational and transactional leaders.

Here it is useful to compare Woodrow Wilson with the first Bush. In the long term, as we saw earlier, Wilson's vision was partially vindicated, but he lacked the leadership skill needed for its execution and implementation in his own time. With Bush 41, the "vision thing" and his educational impact were very limited, but his execution and management were very good. Perhaps the facetious moral of the story is that at some mythical day in the future, genetic engineers will be able to produce leaders equally endowed with both sets of skills. Comparing the two Bushes, who shared half their genes, makes it is clear that nature has not yet solved the problem.

This is not an argument against transformational leaders in general. As I argued earlier, leaders such as Gandhi, Mandela, or King can play crucial roles in transforming a people's identity and aspirations. Nor is this an argument against transformational leaders in American foreign policy. Franklin Roosevelt and Truman made crucial contributions to the creation of the American era, and others, such as Nixon with his opening to China or Carter with his emphasis on human rights and nuclear nonproliferation, have reoriented other important aspects of foreign policy. But in judging leaders we need to pay attention to both acts of omission and acts of commission; both things that happened and things that did not happen; dogs that barked and those that did not.

As Gautam Mukunda observes, "Despite the positive connotations of the word innovation, most innovations fail. Extreme leaders are important because they make choices most leaders would not make."[26] A key question is how much risk democratic followers want their leaders to take in foreign policy, and that depends very much on the context. The big problem in foreign policy is the complexity of the context, where one has to understand not only international and transnational systemic effects, but the intricacies of domestic politics in multiple societies. This additional complexity gives special relevance to the Aristotelian virtue of prudence—avoiding excess or deficiency. We live in a world of diverse cultures and know very little about social engineering and how to "build nations." When we cannot be sure how to improve the world, prudence becomes an important virtue, and hubristic visions can pose a grave danger. In foreign policy as in medicine, it is important to start with the Hippocratic oath: first, do no harm. For these reasons, the virtues of transactional leaders with good contextual intelligence are very important. A Bush 41 without the ability to articulate a vision but able to steer successfully through crises turns out to be a better leader than a Bush 43 with a powerful vision but little contextual intelligence.

In trying to explain the role of secretary of state, George Shultz once compared it to gardening—"the constant nurturing of a complex array of actors, interests and goals." But Shultz's Stanford colleague and eventual successor, Condoleezza Rice, wanted a more transformational diplomacy, "not accepting the world as it is, but trying to change it. Rice's ambition is not just to be a gardener—she wants to be a landscape architect."[27] There is a role for both, depending on the context, but we should avoid the common mistake of automatically thinking that the transformational landscape architect is a better leader than the careful gardener. Good leadership in this century may or may not be transformational, but it will require a careful understanding of the context of change.

The Context of American Power in the Twenty-First Century

We have looked at how eight presidents—transformational and transactional leaders alike—presided over the creation of an unparalleled American primacy by the end of the twentieth century, and how the first two presidents of this century handled it. Will it last? Certainly not in the form it took in the last century. The National Intelligence Council projects that "by 2030, no country—whether the US, China, or any other large country—will be a hegemonic power."[28] As James Mann, the author of books about both George W. Bush and Barack Obama, has observed, "The Vulcans of the Bush era reflected a belief in overwhelming American power, one that was linked to the years immediately after the end of the Cold War. . . . Obama's time in office has marked the beginning of a new era in America's relations with the rest of the world, an era when American primacy is no longer taken for granted."[29] Whether Mann is correct that 2003 represented the outer limits of American power or simply another turn in cycles of hubris cannot be known at this time, but whatever the answer, the twenty-first century is encountering two major power shifts to which American leaders will have to adjust. One is power transition among countries, from West to East, and the other is power diffusion from governments to nongovernmental actors, regardless of whether it is East or West.[30]

The issue of power transition is sometimes called the rise of Asia, but it should more properly be called the recovery of Asia and the rise of the rest. What we will see in the twenty-first century is the recovery of Asia to its normal proportions, with more than half of the world's population and more than half of the world's product, as it was in 1750 before the Industrial Revolution in the West.

Power diffusion is best understood in terms of the way technologies, and particularly information technology, are affecting the costs and reducing the barriers to entry in participating in international affairs. What this means is that things once restricted to very large organizations like governments or corporations are now available to anyone, and this has a significant impact on world politics. It does not mean that the governments are being replaced or that the nation-state is obsolete. Rather, it means that the stage on which governments act is now crowded with many more smaller actors. The cyber domain is a good example.

Regarding the issue of power transition from West to East, the Bush administration did not ignore Asia, but neither did it not focus resources or attention on the fastest growing part of the globe. Instead, partly in reaction to 9/11 and partly because of the Bush Doctrine, in the first decade of this century the United States spent the largest part of its resources on one of the poorest parts of the globe. In 2011 the Obama administration announced that it would "pivot" its foreign policy toward a greater concentration on Asia, though it later changed that terminology to "rebalance" so that Europe, the Middle East, and other regions would not feel neglected.

In Asia, China will most likely pass the United States in the total size of its economy within a decade or so, but if one looks also at military and soft power resources, the United States will remain more powerful than China for the next few decades. Why does it matter? Too much power can lead to hubris, and mistaken strategy, but it is very important to have accurate perceptions about the distribution of power. When people are too worried about power transitions, they may overreact or follow strategies that are dangerous. As Thucydides described it, the Peloponnesian War in which the Greek city-state system tore itself apart was caused by the rise in the power of Athens and the fear it created in Sparta. Similarly, World War I, which destroyed the centrality of the European state system in the world, is often said to have been caused by the rise in the power of Germany and the fear that created in Britain (though the causes were actually much more complex).

Some analysts predict that will be the story of power in the twenty-first century: the rise in the power of China will create fear in the United States, which will lead to a great conflict, but that is bad history and a poor understanding of power for our century. By 1900 Germany had already passed Britain in industrial strength. In other words, the United States has more time than Britain had, and it does not have to be as fearful. If we are too fearful, both sides may overreact. Chinese—thinking America is in decline— push too hard, and Americans, fearing the rise of China, overreact. That is the danger we face in power transition, and the best way to avoid that is by having a clear-eyed view of all dimensions of power and how it is changing and the fact that we do not have to be so fearful.

The other reason why it is important not to be too fearful is the diffusion of power. What we are seeing is that both China and the United States, and of course Europe, Japan, and others, will be facing a new set of transnational challenges—issues like climate change, transnational terrorism, cyber insecurity, pandemics. All these issues, which will increase in the future, are going to require cooperation. Obama's 2010 National Security Strategy referred to the fact that we have to think of power as positive-sum, not just zero-sum.[31] In other words, there may be times when it is good for the United States (and for the world) if Chinese power increases. Take, for example, China's power to control its greenhouse gas emissions, the one area where China is an undoubted superpower. We should be eager to see China increase its capacities in that area. This is win-win. Many of the new transnational challenges that we face are areas where we have to get away from just thinking about power *over* others and think about power *with* others. That is another reason why we do not want to become so fearful that we are not able to cooperate with China. Leaders are facing a world that will be quite different from the world of the nineteenth or twentieth century. Leadership skills, particularly contextual intelligence, will be crucial as the United States adjusts to these twenty-first-century structural changes.

Secretary of State Hillary Clinton referred to the Obama administration's policy in its first term as based on smart power, which combines hard and soft power resources. She said we should not talk about multipolarity; we should talk about multipartnerships. This is a different approach to the future of power in the twenty-first century. Franklin Roosevelt, at the time of the Great Depression, said, "We have nothing to fear but fear itself." In the twenty-first century, leaders will have to educate their followers that one of the most worrisome things is fear itself. If we can keep a balanced appraisal of the distribution of power and figure out ways to deal with the common challenges that we face, we can indeed have win-win situations. Successful leaders will need to get away from old ways of thinking about power and educate their followers about a broader understanding of power to be able to accommodate the changes that are going to occur in this twenty-first century.

Elsewhere I have likened the context of politics today to a three-dimensional chess game in which interstate military power is highly concentrated in the United States; interstate economic power is distributed in a multipolar manner among the United States, the European Union, Japan, and the BRICS (Brazil, Russia, India, China, and South Africa); and power over transnational issues like climate change, crime, terror, and pandemics is highly diffused. Assessing the distribution of resources among actors varies with each domain. The structure of power in this world is neither unipolar, multipolar, nor chaotic—it is all three at the same time. Thus a smart grand strategy must be able to handle very different distributions of power in different domains and understand the trade-offs between them. It makes no more sense to see the world through a purely realist lens that focuses only on the top chessboard or through a liberal institutional lens that looks primarily at the other boards. Contextual intelligence for today's leaders will require a new synthesis of "liberal realism" that looks at all three boards at the same time. After all, in a three-level game, a player who focuses only on one board is bound to lose in the long run.

That will require an understanding of how to exercise power *with* as well as power *over* other states. On issues arising on the top board of interstate military relations, an understanding of ways to form alliances and balance power will remain crucial. But the best order of military battle will do little good in solving many of the problems on the bottom chessboard, such as pandemics or climate change, even though these issues can present threats to the security of millions of people on the order of magnitude of military threats that traditionally drive national strategies. Leadership on such issues will require cooperation, institutions, and pursuit of public goods from which all can benefit and none can be excluded.

Any net assessment of American power in the coming decades remains uncertain. There is always a range of possible futures, not one. Regarding American power relative to China, much will depend on the uncertainties of future political change in China. Barring such political uncertainties, China's size and high rate of economic growth will almost certainly increase its relative strength vis-à-vis the United States. This will bring it closer to the United States in power resources, but as Singapore's Lee Kwan Yew has pointed out, it does not necessarily mean that China will surpass the United States as the most powerful country. Even if China suffers no major domestic political setback, projections based on GDP growth alone are one dimensional and ignore US military and soft power advantages, as well as China's geopolitical disadvantages in the internal Asian balance of power.

Looking to the future, Anne-Marie Slaughter argues that America's culture of openness and innovation will keep it central in a world where networks supplement if not fully replace hierarchical power. The United States is well placed to benefit from such networks and alliances if its leaders follow smart strategies. In structural terms, it matters that the two entities in the world with per capita income and sophisticated economies similar to the American economy—Europe and Japan—are both allied to the United States. In traditional realist terms of balances of power resources, that makes a large difference for the net position of American power, but only if our leaders maintain the alliances and institutional cooperation. In addition, in a more positive sum view of power *with* rather than *over* other countries, Europe and Japan provide the largest pools of resources for dealing with common transnational problems.

On question of absolute rather than relative American decline, the United States faces serious domestic problems in areas like debt, secondary education, and political gridlock, but one should note that they are only part of the picture. The United States leads in top universities, innovation, research and development, and twenty-first-century technologies such as nano and biotechnology. It is one of the few rich countries that does not face a demographic challenge of declining population, and it is becoming increasingly self-sufficient in energy resources. As Eisenhower made clear, American foreign policy rests on strength at home, and Obama has frequently reiterated that position.

Of the multiple possible futures, stronger cases can be made for the positive than the negative ones. But among the negative futures, the most plausible is one in which the United States overreacts to terrorist attacks by closing inward and thus cuts itself off from the strength its obtains from openness. But barring such mistaken leadership strategies, in principle and over a longer term, there are solutions to the major American problems that preoccupy us today. Of course, such solutions may forever remain out of reach. But it is important to distinguish hopeless situations where there are no solutions from those that could in principle be solved.

Decline is a misleading metaphor. In the eyes of some, American decline "began in the 1940s. The US reached the peak of its powers in 1945 when it literally had half the world's wealth and production with incredible security."[32] Fortunately Obama has rejected that confusing metaphor and the suggested strategy of managing decline. America is not in absolute decline, and in relative terms there is a reasonable probability that it is likely to remain more powerful than any single state in the coming decades. We do not live in a "post-American world," but neither do we live any longer in the "American era" of the late twentieth century. In terms of primacy, the United States will be "first" but not "sole." No one has a crystal ball, but the National Intelligence Council may be correct in its projection that while the unipolar moment is over, the United States most likely will remain *primus inter pares* among the other great powers in 2030 because of the multifaceted nature of its power and legacies of its leadership.[33]

The United States will be faced with a rise in the power resources of many others—both states and nonstate actors. Presidents will face an increasing number of issues in which obtaining our preferred outcomes will require power *with* others as much as power *over* others. Our leaders' capacity to maintain alliances and create networks will be an important dimension of our hard and soft power. The problem of America's role in the twenty-first century is not one of a poorly specified "decline," but developing the contextual intelligence to understand that even the largest country cannot achieve the outcomes it wants without the help of others. Educating the public to both understand and operate successfully in the context of this global information age will be the real task for presidential leadership.

Chapter 1. The Role of Leadership

1. Stephen Walt, "The End of the American Era," *The National Interest*, October 25, 2011.

2. Henry Kissinger, *Diplomacy* (New York: Simon and Schuster, 1994), 37.

3. Kenneth Waltz, *Man, the State and War* (New York: Columbia University Press, 1954), refers to three "images": the individual, the state, and the international system.

4. Robert H. Wiebe, *The Search for Order: 1877–1920* (New York: Hill and Wang, 1967), 225.

5. Paul Bairoch, "International Industrialization Levels from 1750 to 1980," *Journal of European Economic History* 11 (Spring 1982): 275, 284.

6. For example, the "loss of China," the Soviet A–bomb, stalemate in Korea, and the rise of Castro. For details see Joseph Nye, *The Future of Power* (New York: Public Affairs, 2011), 154–55.

7. See G. John Ikenberry, *Liberal Leviathan: The Origins, Crisis and Transformation of the American World Order* (Princeton: Princeton University Press, 2011).

8. J. Richard Hackman, *Leading Teams: Setting the Stage for Great Performance* (Boston: Harvard Business School Press, 2002).

9. Philip Stephens, "Ten Years on, a New Set of Rules," *Financial Times*, May 1, 2007.

10. See Robert C. Tucker, *Politics as Leadership*, rev. ed. (Columbia: University of Missouri Press, 1995), 30.

11. Kissinger, *Diplomacy*, 52.

12. James MacGregor Burns, *Leadership* (New York: Harper and Row, 1978). Burns distinguishes "leaders" from "power wielders," and thus Hitler is not a leader in Burns's terminology. But even power wielders require some inner core of followers, and this value-laden definition hinders analysis of bad leaders. See Barbara Kellerman, *Bad Leadership* (Boston: Harvard Business School Press, 2004).

13. Burns later added another word—"transforming"—to refer to leaders' effects on their followers. James MacGregor Burns, *Transforming Leadership: A New Pursuit of Happiness* (New York: Atlantic Monthly Press, 2003).

14. On the definition and problems of "charismatic," see Joseph S. Nye, *The Powers to Lead* (New York: Oxford University Press, 2008), 53–61.

15. David G. Winter, "Leader Appeal, Leader Performance, and the Motive Profiles of Leaders and Followers: A Study of American Presidents and Elections," *Journal of Personality and Social Psychology* 52, 1 (1989): 196–202; Dean K. Simonton, "Presidential Greatness: The Historical Consensus and its Psychological Significance," *Political Psychology* 7 (1986): 259–83; and "Dispositional Attributions of (Presidential) Leadership: An Experimental Simulation of Historiometric Results," *Journal of Experimental Social Psychology* 22 (1986): 389–418.

16. Robert J. Sternberg, "Successful Intelligence: A New Approach to Leadership," in *Multiple Intelligences and Leadership*, ed. Ronald E. Riggio et al. (Mahwah, NJ: Lawrence Erlbaum, 2002), 9–28.

17. Robert Rotberg, *Transformative Political Leadership: Making a Difference in the Developing World* (Chicago: University of Chicago Press, 2012), 161.

18. Edward S. Corwin, *The President: Office and Powers, 1787–1957* (New York: NYU Press, 1957), 171.

19. James MacGregor Burns and Georgia J. Sorensen, *Dead Center: Clinton–Gore Leadership and the Perils of Moderation* (New York: Scribner, 1999), 292.

20. "Built to Last," *Economist*, November 26, 2011, 80, cites the business leadership analyst Jim Collins warning that those "who encourage companies to tear themselves apart in the name of 'transformation' have caused terrible harm."

21. Personal conversation with Lee Kuan Yew, January 19, 2012.

22. Alan J. P. Taylor, *Bismarck: The Man and the Statesman* (London: Sutton, 1955), 115.

23. For details see chapter 4, "Contextual Intelligence," in Nye, *The Powers to Lead*.

24. For the debate about whether Kennedy would have extricated the United States from Vietnam had he lived and been elected to a second term, see James Blight, Janet M. Lang, and David A.

Welch, *Vietnam If Kennedy Had Lived: Virtual JFK* (United States: Roman and Littlefield, 2009).

25. See Leslie H. Gelb, *Power Rules* (New York: Harper Collins, 2009).

26. Robert W. Tucker, *The Purposes of American Power: An Essay on National Security* (New York: Praeger, 1981), 3.

27. Quoted in Robert Jervis, *The Meaning of the Nuclear Revolution: Statecraft and the Prospect of Armageddon* (Ithaca: Cornell University Press, 1989), 102.

28. Quoted in Richard Reeves, *President Nixon: Alone in the White House* (New York: Simon and Schuster, 2001), 343.

29. Nigel Bowles, *Nixon's Business: Authority and Power in Presidential Politics* (College Station: Texas A&M Press, 2005), 193.

30. Ibid., 248.

Chapter 2. The Creation of the American Era from Theodore Roosevelt to George H. W. Bush

1. Wiebe, *The Search for Order*, 232–34; Evan Thomas, *The War Lovers: Roosevelt, Lodge, Hearst, and the Rush to Empire, 1898* (New York: Little, Brown, 2010).

2. Ernest May, *American Imperialism: A Speculative Essay* (New York: Atheneum, 1968), 165–66.

3. Wiebe, *The Search for Order*, 250.

4. William N. Tilchin, "Power and Principle: The Statecraft of Theodore Roosevelt," in *Ethics and Statecraft: The Moral Dimensions of International Affairs*, 2nd ed., ed. Cathal J. Nolan (Westport, CT: Praeger, 2004), 115.

5. Kissinger, *Diplomacy*, 54.

6. James Chace, *1912: Wilson, Roosevelt, Taft and Debs—The Election That Changed the Country* (New York: Simon and Schuster, 2004), 108.

7. Donald F. Anderson, *William Howard Taft: A Conservative's Conception of the Presidency* (Ithaca: Cornell University Press, 1968), 34.

8. Ibid., 24–25.

9. David H. Burton, *William Howard Taft: Confident Peacemaker* (Philadelphia: St. Joseph's University Press, 2004) 92, 95.

10. Anderson, *William Howard Taft*, 27.

11. Ibid., 84.

12. Burton, *William Howard Taft*, 145.

13. Ibid., 63.

14. Anderson, *William Howard Taft*, 279.

15. Quoted in Inis Claude, *Power and International Relations* (New York: Random House, 1962), 81.

16. John Milton Cooper, Jr., *Woodrow Wilson: A Biography* (New York: Knopf, 2009), 287.

17. Ernest R. May, *The World War and American Isolation, 1914–1917* (Chicago: Quadrangle, 1959), 428–37.

18. Thomas J. Knock, *To End All Wars: Woodrow Wilson and the Quest for a New World Order* (Princeton: Princeton University Press, 1992), 33.

19. Erez Manela, *The Wilsonian Moment: Self Determination and the International Origins of Anticolonial Nationalism* (Oxford: Oxford University Press, 2007), 47–48.

20. See Margaret MacMillan, *Paris 1919: Six Months That Changed the World* (New York: Random House, 2001).

21. See Robert Dallek, *Franklin D. Roosevelt and American Foreign Policy, 1932–1945* (New York: Oxford University Press, 1979), 548.

22. Barbara Farnham, *Roosevelt and the Munich Crisis: A Study of Political Decision–Making* (Princeton: Princeton University Press, 1997), 49.

23. Ibid., 50.

24. Simon Kuznets, *Economic Growth and Structure* (New York: Norton, 1965), 144.

25. David K. Adams, "The Concept of Parallel Action: FDR's Internationalism in a Decade of Isolationism," in *From Theodore Roosevelt to FDR: Internationalism and Isolationism in American Foreign Policy* (Staffordshire, UK: Keele University Press, 1995), 115; Steven Casey, *Cautious Crusade: Franklin D. Roosevelt, American Public Opinion, and the War against Nazi Germany* (New York: Oxford University Press, 2001), 23; Adam J. Berinsky, *In a Time of War: Understanding American Public Opinion from World War II to Iraq* (Chicago: University of Chicago Press, 2009), 46.

26. Lynne Olson, *Citizens of London: The Americans Who Stood with Britain in Its Darkest, Finest Hour* (New York: Random House, 2010), 67.

27. Quoted in Michael Fullilove, *Rendezvous with Destiny: How Franklin D. Roosevelt and Five Extraordinary Men Took America into the War and Into the World* (New York: Penguin, 2013), 23.

28. Quoted in Farnham, *Roosevelt and the Munich Crisis*, 43.

29. Dallek, *Franklin D. Roosevelt*, 312.

30. Ibid., 274.

31. Marc Trachtenberg, *The Craft of International History: A Guide to Method* (Princeton: Princeton University Press, 2006), 79–139, places more emphasis on design than on ineptitude.

32. Jonathan G. Utley, *Going to War with Japan, 1937–1941* (Knoxville: University of Tennessee Press, 1985), 179–80.

33. David McCullough, *Truman* (New York: Simon and Schuster, 1992), 141.

34. George H. Gallup, *The Gallup Poll: Public Opinion 1935–1971* (New York: Random House, 1972), 1:534–35.

35. Ibid., 534.

36. Robert Shapiro, "The Legacy of the Marshall Plan: American Public Support for Foreign Aid," in *The Marshall Plan: Fifty Years After*, ed. Martin A. Schain (New York: Palgrave, 2001), 270.

37. Ernest R. May, "The Nature of Foreign Policy: The Calculated versus the Axiomatic," *Daedalus* 91, 4 (1962): 653–67.

38. William Taubman, *Stalin's American Policy* (Toronto: George J. McLeod, 1982), 100.

39. Walter Isaacson and Evan Thomas, *The Wise Men: Six Friends and the World They Made* (New York: Simon and Schuster), 376.

40. Robert Dallek, *The American Style of Foreign Policy: Cultural Politics and Foreign Affairs* (New York: Knopf, 1983), 157.

41. Isaacson and Thomas, *The Wise Men*, 407.

42. Alonzo Hamby, "Truman Defeats Kennan: The Lines Are Drawn for the Postwar World," *Weekly Standard*, October 23, 2006, 37.

43. Geir Lundestad, *Empire by Integration: The United States and European Integration, 1945–1997* (Oxford: Oxford University Press, 1998), 155.

44. John Lewis Gaddis, *George F. Kennan: An American Life* (New York: Penguin, 2012), 495.

45. Ole R. Holsti, *Public Opinion and American Foreign Policy* (Ann Arbor: University of Michigan Press, 1996), 31.

46. Ibid., 132.

47. Gallup, *The Gallup Poll*, 1262.

48. Ibid., 1259.

49. Ibid., 1345.

50. Ibid., 1243.

51. Fredrik Logevall, *Embers of War: The Fall of an Empire and the Making of America's Vietnam* (New York: Random House, 2012), 508–9.

52. "The Decline of U.S. Power," *Businessweek*, March 12, 1979, 37.

53. Robert W. Tucker, *The Purposes of American Power* (New York: Praeger, 1981), 5.

54. "The Reagan Legacy: He Led a Revolution. Will It Survive?" *Economist*, June 12, 2004.

55. Quoted in Henry Nau, "Ronald Reagan," in *Presidents, American Democracy Promotion and World Order*, ed. Michael Cox, Timothy J. Lynch, and Nicolas Bouchet (New York: Routledge, 2013).

56. As his notes and correspondence show, Reagan was not bereft of foreign policy ideas, but various participants in his administration have confirmed that he was often weak on their operational implications. See Kiron K. Skinner, Annelise Aderson, and Martin Anderson, *Reagan: A Life in Letters* (New York: Free Press, 2003).

57. David M. Abshire, *Saving the Reagan Presidency: Trust Is the Coin of the Realm* (College Station: Texas A&M University Press, 2005), 200.

58. Jack F. Matlock, personal conversations. See also Matlock, *Reagan and Gorbachev: How the Cold War Ended* (New York: Random House, 2004), 327.

59. Quoted in Stephen Sestanovich, "Gorbachev's Foreign Policy: A Diplomacy of Decline," *Problems of Communism* (January–February 1988): 2.

60. Mary E. Sarotte, "In Victory, Magnanimity: US Foreign Policy, 1989–91, and the Legacy of Prefabricated Multilateralism," *International Politics* 48, 4/5 (2011): 94. See also Mary E. Sarotte, *1989: The Struggle to Create Post–Cold War Europe* (Princeton: Princeton University Press, 2009).

61. Zbigniew Brzezinski, *Second Chance* (New York: Basic Books, 2007).

62. Philip Zelikow and Condoleezza Rice, *Germany Unified and Europe Transformed: A Study in Statecraft* (Cambridge: Harvard University Press, 1997), 21.

63. Alexander L. George and Juliette L. George, *Woodrow Wilson and Colonel House: A Personality Study* (New York: Dover, 1964), 114.

64. See Philip E. Tetlock and Aaron Belkin, eds., *Counterfactual Thought Experiments in World Politics* (Princeton: Princeton University Press, 1996).

65. Quoted in Anderson, *William Howard Taft*, 288.

66. Chace, *1912*.

67. Philip Roth, *The Plot Against America* (New York: Houghton Mifflin, 2004).

68. Ian Toll, "A Reluctant Enemy," *New York Times*, December 7, 2011.

69. Fullilove, *Rendezvous with Destiny*, 358.

70. Trachtenberg, *The Craft of International History*, 79–139.

71. See William Langer and S. Everett Gleason, *The Undeclared War, 1940–41* (New York: Harper, 1953).

72. Bruce M. Russett, *No Clear and Present Danger: A Skeptical View of the United States Entry into World War II* (Boulder: Westview Press, 1997), 27.

73. Taubman, *Stalin's American Policy*, 36.

74. Frank Costigliola, *Roosevelt's Lost Alliances: How Personal Politics Helped Start the Cold War* (Princeton: Princeton University Press, 2012), 420, 422.

75. Hamby, "Truman Defeats Kennan," 37.

76. Zelikow and Rice, *Germany Unified and Europe Transformed*, pvi.

77. For details, see Nye, *The Powers to Lead*, 3–5.

Chapter 3. Ethics and Good Foreign Policy Leadership

1. See, for example, MacGregor Burns, *Leadership*, 18. For discussion see Joanne B. Ciulla, *Ethics: The Heart of Leadership*, 2nd ed. (Westport, CT: Praeger, 2004).

2. David Brooks, "If It Feels Right . . . ," *New York Times*, September 13, 2011.

3. "Infallible," *Economist*, December 21, 2002, 23.

4. Isaiah Berlin, *Historical Inevitability*, August Comte Memorial Trust Lecture (London: Oxford University Press, 1954), 26, 78.

5. S. Alexander Haslam and Michael J. Platow, "The Link between Leadership and Followership: How Affirming Social Identity Translates Vision into Action," *Personality and Social Psychology Bulletin* 27, 11 (2001): 1471.

6. The problem of dirty hands has had various formulations. Joseph Badaracco describes it in terms of conflicting moral principles, or "right vs. right." See his *Defining Moments: When Managers Must Choose between Right and Right* (Boston: Harvard Business School Press, 1997). I focus more on the trade-off between principles and consequences and the tragic choices that arise because there is "no single standard that renders all moral values commensurable." See Kenneth I. Winston, "Necessity and Choice in Political Ethics: Varieties of Dirty Hands," in *Professional Ethics and Social Responsibility*, ed. Daniel E. Wueste (Lanham, MD: Rowman and Littlefield, 1994), 37–66. Gerald F. Gaus tries to dissolve this problem, but I do not regard it as a satisfactory solution. See "Dirty Hands," in *A Companion to Applied Ethics*, ed. R. G. Frey and Christopher Heath Wellman (Malden, MA: Blackwell, 2003), 167–79.

7. Michael Walzer, "Political Action: The Problem of Dirty Hands," *Philosophy and Public Affairs* 2 (1973): 164.

8. Max Weber, "Politics as a Vocation," in *From Max Weber: Essays in Sociology*, ed. H. H. Gerth and C. Wright Mills (New York: Oxford University Press, 1958), 126.

9. Stuart Hampshire, quoted in Badaracco, *Defining Moments*, 52.

10. Tom Beauchamp, *Philosophical Ethics: An Introduction to Moral Philosophy* (New York: McGraw Hill, 1982), 179.

11. McCullough, *Truman*, 443

12. Samuel Walker, "Recent Literature on Truman's Atomic Bomb Decision: A Search for Middle Ground," *Diplomatic History* 29, 2 (April 2005): 333.

13. Harry S. Truman, "Farewell Address to the American People," January 15, 1953, in *American Presidents: Farewell Messages to the Nation, 1796–2001*, ed. Gleaves Whitney (Lanham, MD: Lexington Books, 2003), 393–98.

14. Kenneth Winston discusses this as a case of dirty hands in a yet unpublished manuscript.

15. "Philosophy and Neuroscience: Posing the Right Question," *Economist*, March 24, 2007, 92.

16. See Winston, "Necessity and Choice in Political Ethics."

17. Isaiah Berlin, "Two Concepts of Liberty," in *Liberty: Incorporating Four Essays on Liberty*, ed. Henry Hardy (New York: Oxford University Press, 1969), 168.

18. Amartya Sen, *The Idea of Justice* (Cambridge: Harvard University Press, 2009), 12.

19. George C. Edwards III, *On Deaf Ears: The Limits of the Bully Pulpit* (New Haven: Yale University Press, 2003).

20. Graham T. Allison and Lance M. Liebman, "Lying in Office," in *Ethics and Politics: Cases and Comments*, 2nd ed., ed. Amy Gutmann and Dennis Thompson (Chicago: Nelson–Hall, 1990), 41.

21. Cathal J. Nolan, "Bodyguard of Lies': Franklin D. Roosevelt and Defensible Deceit in World War II," in Nolan, *Ethics and Statecraft*, 35.

22. John Mearsheimer, *Why Leaders Lie* (Oxford: Oxford University Press, 2011), viii.

23. Allison and Liebman, "Lying in Office," 40.

24. Eric Alterman, *When Presidents Lie: A History of Official Deception and Its Consequences* (New York: Viking, 2004), 314.

25. See the arguments in Sisella Bok, *Lying: Moral Choice in Public and Private Life* (New York: Pantheon, 1978).

26. Niccolo Machiavelli, *The Prince*, cited in Badaracco, *Defining Moments*, 110.

27. Bernard Williams, *Moral Luck* (Cambridge: Cambridge University Press, 1981), 26.

28. James Hershberg, quoted in Michael Abramowitz, "Truman's Trials Resonate for Bush," *Washington Post*, December 15, 2006, A3.

29. David Brooks, "Heroes and History," *New York Times*, July 17, 2007, A21.

30. Abramowitz, "Truman's Trials Resonate for Bush."

31. Russell Hardin, "Morals for Public Officials," in *Moral Leadership: The Theory and Practice of Power, Judgment, and Policy*, ed. Deborah L. Rhode (San Francisco: Jossey–Bass, 2006), 116–17.

32. Philip G. Zimbardo, "The Psychology of Power: To the Person? To the Situation? To the System?" in Rhode, *Moral Leadership*, 153.

33. See Stanley Hoffmann, *Duties Beyond Borders: On the Limits and Possibilities of Ethical International Politics* (Syracuse: Syracuse University Press, 1981).

34. See Steven Pinker, *The Better Angels of Our Nature: Why Violence Has Declined* (New York: Penguin, 2011); and Joshua S. Goldstein, *Winning the War on War: The Decline of Armed Conflict Worldwide* (New York: Dutton, 2011).

35. Charles Guthrie and Michael Quinlan, *Just War: The Just War Tradition: Ethics in Modern Warfare* (New York: Walker, 2007). See also my discussion in Joseph Nye, *Nuclear Ethics* (New York: Basic Books, 1986).

36. Hans Morgenthau and Arnold Wolfers are classic examples of realist normative analysis; John Rawls and Michael Walzer are examples of liberal normative thought; Charles Beitz is an example of a cosmopolitan analysis.

37. Walter Russell Mead, *Special Providence: American Foreign Policy and How It Changed the World* (New York: Routledge, 2002).

38. See Gary J. Bass, *Freedom's Battle: The Origins of Humanitarian Intervention* (New York: Knopf, 2008), 3.

39. See Samantha Power, *A Problem From Hell: America and the Age of Genocide* (New York: Basic Books, 2002).

40. Kwame Anthony Appiah, *The Ethics of Identity* (Princeton: Princeton University Press, 2005), 235.

41. Winston, "Necessity and Choice in Political Ethics," 49.

42. Arnold Wolfers, "Statemanship and Moral Choice," in *Discord and Collaboration: Essays on International Politics* (Baltimore: Johns Hopkins University Press, 1965), 51.

43. Robert H. Jackson, "The Situational Ethics of Statecraft," in Nolan, *Ethics and Statecraft*, 27.

44. John Rawls, *The Law of Peoples* (Cambridge: Harvard University Press, 1999); Michael Doyle, "One World, Many Peoples: International Justice in John Rawls' The Law of Peoples," *Perspectives on Politics* 4, 1 (March 2006): 109–20.

45. Winston, "Necessity and Choice in Political Ethics," 50.

46. James MacGregor Burns and Susan Dunn, *The Three Roosevelts: Patrician Leaders Who Transformed America* (New York: Grove Press, 2001), 102.

47. Kathleen Dalton, *Theodore Roosevelt: A Strenuous Life* (New York: Knopf, 2002), 300.

48. Chace, *1912*, 262.

49. MacGregor Burns and Dunn, *The Three Roosevelts*, 45.

50. Quoted in James Bradley, *The Imperial Cruise: A Secret History of Empire and War* (New York: Little, Brown, 2009), 162, 98.

51. Tilchin, "Power and Principle," 97.

52. Warren Zimmerman, *The First Great Triumph: How Five Americans Made Their Country A Great Power* (New York: Farrar, Straus and Giroux, 2002), 409, 417; see also Dalton, *Theodore Roosevelt*, 227–29.

53. Dalton, *Theodore Roosevelt*, 323.

54. Quoted in Zimmerman, *The First Great Triumph*, 434–36.

55. Tilchin, "Power and Principle," 115.

56. Anderson, *William Howard Taft*, 1.

57. John Morton Blum, *Woodrow Wilson and the Politics of Morality* (Boston: Little Brown, 1956), 7–9.

58. Alexander L. George and Juliette L. George, *Woodrow Wilson and Colonel House* (New York: Dover, 1956), 114–15.

59. Cooper, *Woodrow Wilson*, 5.

60. Manela, *The Wilsonian Moment*, 41, 215.

61. Cooper, *Woodrow Wilson*, 6.

62. Arthur Link, "The Higher Realism of Woodrow Wilson," in Nolan, *Ethics and Statecraft*, 127–31.

63. Manela, *The Wilsonian Moment*, 225.

64. Blum, *Woodrow Wilson and the Politics of Morality*, 199.

65. Gary Wills, *Certain Trumpets: The Nature of Leadership* (New York: Simon and Schuster, 1994), 27–30.

66. Cathal Nolan, "Bodyguard of Lies," 37, 50, 53.

67. Alonzo Hamby, "Harry S. Truman: Insecurity and Responsibility," in *Leadership in the Modern Presidency*, ed. Fred I. Greenstein (Cambridge: Harvard University Press, 1988), 42.

68. Bronwyn Fryer, "Timeless Leadership: A Conversation with David McCullough," *Harvard Business Review* (March 2008): 3.

69. Hamby, "Harry S. Truman," 64.

70. Stephen Ambrose, *Eisenhower: The President* (New York: Simon and Schuster, 1984), 2:11, 17.

71. Fred I. Greenstein, *The Presidential Difference: Leadership Style from FDR to George W. Bush*, 2nd ed. (Princeton: Princeton University Press, 2004), 57.

72. Ambrose, *Eisenhower*, 620–22, 625.

73. Ibid., 626.

74. Dwight Eisenhower, *Mandate for Change, 1953–1956* (New York: New American Library, 1963), 510.

75. Jean Edward Smith, *Eisenhower in War and Peace* (New York: Random House, 2012), xiii.

76. Ambrose, *Eisenhower*, 206.

77. Fred I. Greenstein, *The Hidden-Hand Presidency: Eisenhower as Leader* (New York: Basic Books, 1982), 69.

78. Ibid.

79. All quotes from "The Man Who Beat Communism" and "The Reagan Legacy," *Economist*, June 24, 2004, 13, 24, 25.

80. David Gergen, *Eyewitness to Power: The Essence of Leadership* (New York: Simon and Schuster, 2000), 153.

81. Quoted in Greenstein, *The Hidden-Hand Presidency*, 145.

82. Peter Schweizer, *The Bushes: Portrait of a Dynasty* (New York: Doubleday, 2004).

83. Nicholas Burns, "Our Best Foreign Policy President," *Boston Globe*, December 9, 2011.

84. George Bush and Brent Scowcroft, *A World Transformed* (New York: Vintage Books, 1998), xiii–xiv.

85. Zelikow and Rice, *Germany Unified and Europe Transformed*, 29.

86. Ibid., 95, 105.

87. Burns, "Our Best Foreign Policy President."

88. For examples, see Giulio Gallaroti, *The Power Curse: Influence and Illusion in World Politics* (Boulder: Lynne Rienner, 2009).

89. Jack Goldsmith, *Power and Constraint: The Accountable Presidency after 9/11* (New York: Norton, 2102).

90. See, for example, Chalmers Johnson, *The Sorrows of Empire: Militarism, Secrecy, and the End of the Republic* (New York: Henry Holt, 2004); Andrew J. Bacevic, *American Empire: The Realities and Consequences of U.S. Diplomacy* (Cambridge: Harvard University Press, 2002).

91. See Charles P. Kindleberger, "Dominance and Leadership in the International Economy: Exploitation, Public Goods, and Free Rides," *International Studies Quarterly* 25, 2 (June 1981): 242–54; Michael Mandelbaum, *The Case for Goliath: How America Acts as the World's Government in the Twenty-First Century* (New York: Public Affairs, 2005); Robert Kagan, *The World America Made* (New York: Knopf, 2012).

92. See G. John Ikenberry, *Liberal Leviathan: The Origins, Crisis, and Transformation of the American World Order* (Princeton: Princeton University Press, 2011); and Samuel P. Huntington, *The Third Wave: Democratization in the Late Twentieth Century* (Norman, University of Oklahoma Press, 1991).

CHAPTER 4. TWENTY-FIRST-CENTURY LEADERSHIP

1. John Lewis Gaddis, *Surprise, Security, and the American Experience* (Cambridge: Harvard University Press, 2004), 77.

2. Brzezinski, *Second Chance.*

3. George W. Bush, *Decision Points* (New York: Crown, 2010), 397.

4. Gaddis, *Surprise, Security, and the American Experience*, 93.

5. This does not mean that all Bush's policies were failures. Indeed some, like his approach to AIDS in Africa, were both innovative and transformational.

6. Personal conversation with Brent Scowcroft, May 2003.

7. MacMillan, *Paris 1919*, 10.

8. David Rothkopf, *Running the World: The Inside Story of the National Security Council and the Architects of American Power* (New York: Public Affairs, 2005), 33.

9. Quoted in Stephen F. Knott, *Rush to Judgment: George W. Bush, The War on Terror, and His Critics* (Lawrence: University of Kansas Press, 2012), 164.

10. Hugh Heclo, "The Political Ethos of George Bush," in *The George W. Bush Presidency: An Early Appraisal*, ed. Fred Greenstein (Baltimore: Johns Hopkins University Press, 2003), 48–49.

11. Farnham, *Roosevelt and the Munich Crisis*, 42.

12. Personal conversation with Bob Woodward, August 10, 2005.

13. Bush, *Decision Points*, 272.

14. David E. Sanger, *Confront and Conceal: Obama's Secret Wars and Surprising Use of American Power* (New York: Crown, 2012), 101.

15. George C. Edwards, III, *Overreach: Leadership in the Obama Presidency* (Princeton: Princeton University Press, 2012), 1.

16. Martin S. Indyk, Kenneth G. Lieberthal, and Michael E. O'Hanlon, *Bending History: Barack Obama's Foreign Policy* (Washington, DC: Brookings Institution Press, 2012), 6.

17. Ibid., 1.

18. Ibid., 21.

19. "Gaffes and Choices," *Economist*, August 4, 2012, 11; David Brooks, "Where Obama Shines," *New York Times*, July 29, 2012.

20. James Fallows, "Obama, Explained," *Atlantic* (March 2012).

21. Fareed Zakaria, "On Foreign Policy, Why Barack Is Like Ike," *TIME*, December 21, 2012. http://ti.me/12zwa5H.

22. This is the argument of James Mann, *The Obamians: The Struggle Inside the White House to Redefine American Power* (New York: Viking, 2012).

23. Sanger, *Confront and Conceal*, 421.

24. Indyk, Lieberthal, and O'Hanlon, *Bending History*, 23.

25. Robert Blackwill, personal communication, August 9, 2012.

26. Gautam Mukunda, *Indispensable: When Leaders Really Matter* (Boston: Harvard Business Review Press, 2012), 1–20.

27. Quoted in Derek Chollet, "Altered State: Rice Aims to Put Foggy Bottom Back on the Map," *Washington Post*, April 7, 2005.

28. Office of the Director of National Intelligence, *Global Trends 2030: Alternative Worlds* (Washington DC, 2012), iii.

29. Mann, *The Obamians*, 345.

30. See Nye, *The Future of Power*.

31. The White House, *National Security Strategy* (Washington, DC, May 2010).

32. "Noam Chomsky in interview," October 28, 2011. www .publicserviceeurope.com/article/1047/professor–noam–chomsky –in–interview.

33. Office of the Director of National Intelligence, *Global Trends 2030: Alternative Worlds* (Washington DC, 2012).

INDEX

Note: Page numbers followed by "t" indicate references to tables.

Abramowitz, Michael, 169n28, 169n30
Abshire, David M., 52, 166n57
Abu Ghraib Prison, 91
accountability, 86
Acheson, Dean, 43–45, 118
Acton, Lord, 133–34
Adams, David K., 164n25
Adams, John Quincy, 94
Adropov, Yuri, 55, 70
Afghanistan, 6, 70, 146, 148
Al Qaeda, 6, 144
Alaska, 24
Alexander the Great, 78
Allison, Graham T., 169n20, 169n23
Alterman, Eric, 86, 169n24
Ambrose, Stephen, 121, 171n70, 171n72, 172n76
American exceptionalism, 3, 24, 26, 35, 45, 65, 75, 93, 133, 135
American primacy, 1, 3, 5, 31, 41, 98, 106, 132–39, 151–52, 159; and George H. W. Bush, 59; and Nixon, 20; and presidential leadership, 14–18, 72–74; and Truman, 43, 45–46, 120
Anderson, Annelise, 166n56
Anderson, Donald F., 163n7, 164n10, 164n14, 167n65, 171n56
Anderson, Martin, 166n56
Andropov, Yuri, 55, 70
apartheid, 73, 127
Appiah, Kwame Anthony, 96, 170n40
Arab league, 147
Arab revolutions, 141, 147

Arab spring. See Arab revolutions
Arbenz, Jacobo, 122
Aristotle, 80, 81
arms control, 16, 123
Attila the Hun, 78
attraction, 9
Augustine, 93
authority, 91, 108; deference to, 77; and Eisenhower, 69; exercise of, 84; institutional, 91; presidential, 104

Bacevic, Andrew J., 172n90,
Badaracco, Joseph L., Jr., 168n6, 168n9, 169n26
Bairoch, Paul, 161n5
Baker, James, 52, 58
balance of payments, 19
balance of power, 3, 15, 15t, 22–25, 31–32, 45, 63, 65, 92–94, 100, 109–10, 157
bargaining, 12, 85; and Reagan, 51, 53, 55, 127; transactional, 8; and Wilson, 110
Bass, Gary J., 170n38
Beauchamp, Tom, 168n10
Beitz, Charles, 170n36
Bell, Sherman, 102
Bentham, Jeremy, 80
Berinsky, Adam J., 164n25
Berlin Airlift, 118
Berlin Wall, 58, 129
Berlin, Isaiah, 83, 167n4, 169n17
Bin Laden, Osama, 81; killing of 144, 147, 148
bipolarity, 18–19, 45, 50, 59, 72, 122, 138
Bismarck, 148, 162n22
Blackwill, Robert, 174n25
Blair, Tony, 94, 142
Blight, James, 162n24

Block, Herbert, 4t
Blum, John Morton, 111, 171n57, 171n64
Boer War, 22
Bohlen, Charles, 44
Bok, Sisella, 169n25
Bosnia, 131, 139
Bowles, Nigel, 163n29
Bradley, James, 170n50
Brazil, 156
Bretton Woods, 19–20, 149
Bricker, John W., 69
Brooks, David, 77, 146, 167n2, 169n29, 173n19
Bryan, William Jennings, 22
Brzezinski, Zbigniew, 57, 140, 166n61, 173n2
Burns, James McGregor, 7, 98, 161n12, 162n13, 162n19, 167n1, 170n46, 170n49
Burns, Nicholas, 132, 172n83, 172n87
Burton, David H., 163n9, 164n12
Bush, George H. W., 15t, 51, 55, 70–72, 74, 87, 89, 133, 134, 138, 139, 146, 147, 149; background of, 55, 62, 128; and George W. Bush, 150–51; communication skills of, 62; and contextual intelligence, 56, 58; and ethical foreign policy leadership, 128–32, 132t; and German unification, 56–58, 129, 148; leadership style of, 55–56, 58–59, 129; objectives of, 56–58, 59, 60–61, 60t; organizational skills of, 56, 59, 91; as transactional, 16, 61, 133, 137. *See also* Gulf War
Bush Doctrine, 140, 153
Bush, George W., 89–90, 144, 145, 152; and Asia, 153; and George H. W. Bush, 150–151; and crisis conditions, 11; "freedom agenda" of, 140, 142; as transformational, 6, 139, 141–43; and Iraq, 76, 89, 102, 140

Caesar, Julius, 78
Cam Rahn Bay, 18

Canada, 30, 101
Caribbean, 31, 38, 63, 107–8, 122
Carter, Jimmy, 15t, 55, 70, 88; and the economy, 20; and human rights, 17, 150
Casey, Steven, 164n25
Casey, William, 52
Castro, Fidel, 121, 161n6
Central America, 52, 107, 122, 127, 134
Central Intelligence Agency, 128
Chace, James, 163n6, 167n66, 170n48
Chafee, Adna, 101–2
charisma, 9, 13t, 162n14; and Taft, 27; and Truman, 43, 116
Chicago, 94
China, 152, 161n6; and George H. W. Bush, 130–31; and Eisenhower, 48, 69; and Nixon, 17–20, 50, 149, 150; and Obama, 145, 146; rising power of, 18, 153–55, 156, 157; and Taft, 30, 64; and Truman, 45, 119
Chollet, Derek, 174n27
Chomsky, Noam, 174n32
Churchill, Winston, 39, 85
Ciulla, Joanne B., 167n2
civil rights, 49, 121
Clayton-Bulwer Treaty, 24
Clemenceau, Georges, 34, 110
Cleveland, Grover, 21, 100
climate change, 146, 154, 156
Clinton, Bill, 8, 9t, 9, 11, 15t, 95, 139–40, 141, 162n19
Clinton, Hillary, 155
coalitions: forming of, 12, 13t; and Gulf War, 56, 128, 131 (*see also* Gulf War); and Reagan, 51; and Obama Doctrine, 147
Cold War, 15t, 42, 68, 71–72, 132, 136, 139, 152; conclusion of 16, 50, 55–57, 62, 70, 89, 91, 128 (*see also* Bush, George H. W.); and Eisenhower, 87, 122; and Reagan, 53–55, 70, 126–127
collective security, 34, 42, 56–57, 109–10, 118
Collins, Jim, 162n20

Colombia, 24, 102–3
Committee on the Present Danger, 50
containment, 15t, 16, 40–41, 45–47, 50, 53, 69, 72, 119, 129, 134
contextual intelligence, 12–14, 61, 71, 87, 89, 97, 151, 155–56, 159, 162n23; and George H. W. Bush, 56, 58, 128; and George W. Bush, 76; and Eisenhower, 46, 49, 122; and Obama, 146–47; and Reagan, 52; and Franklin D. Roosevelt, 36, 38, 40, 66, 115; and Theodore Roosevelt, 23, 63; and Truman, 41, 44, 69; and Wilson, 110–11
Coolidge, Calvin, 15t, 16
Cooper, John Milton, 108, 164n16, 171n59, 171n60
Corwin, Edward S., 11, 162n18
cosmopolitanism, 94, 96, 98, 131, 170n36
Costigliola, Frank, 167n74
Creel, George, 33
Cromwell, Oliver, 78
Cuba, 94, 102. See also Cuban Missile Crisis
Cuban Missile Crisis, 17, 85. See also Cuba
Czechoslovakia, 34

Dallek, Robert, 36, 43, 115, 164n21, 165n29, 165n40
Dalton, Kathleen, 170n47, 171n52, 171n53
Danzig Corridor, 34
détente, 18, 50, 53
Dien Bien Phu, 69, 122, 123
Disraeli, Benjamin, 94
Dominican Republic, 22, 24
Domino Theory, 18, 49, 121, 149
Doyle, Michael, 170n44
Dresden, 82, 119
Dukakis, Michael, 70–71
Dulles, John Foster, 47, 49
Dunn, Susan, 170n46, 170n49

Edwards, George C., III, 85, 144, 169n19, 173n15

Eisenhower, Dwight, 9t, 15t, 46–50, 55, 60t, 60, 69, 72, 74, 128, 146, 147, 148, 158; and American primacy, 134; and Cold War, 87, 89 (see also Cold War); as transactional, 9, 16, 61, 137; and ethical foreign policy leadership, 120–24, 124t; nuclear policy of, 124 (see also nuclear weapons); and Vietnam, 149
emotional intelligence, 12, 13, 51, 56, 61, 110, 117, 121, 130
Ethiopia, 34
European Union, 156

Fallows, James, 146, 173n20
Farnham, Barbara, 143, 164n22, 165n28, 173n11
Ford, Gerald R., 15t, 20
Fourteen Points, 32, 34, 65
France, 25, 30, 37, 40, 92, 107, 148
Frederick the Great, 78
Frost, Robert, 74
Fryer, Bronwyn, 171n68
Fukuyama, Francis, 140
Fulbright, J. William, 133
Fullilove, Michael, 165n27, 167n69

Gaddis, John Lewis, 45, 47, 140, 165n44, 173n1, 173n4
Gallaroti, Giulio, 172n88
Gallup, George H., 37, 41, 48, 165n34, 166n47
Gandhi, Mohandas, 10, 150
Gates, Robert, 59
Gauguin, Paul, 88
Gaus, Gerald F., 168n6
Gelb, Leslie H., 163n25
George, Alexander L., 108, 167n63, 171n58
George, Juliette L., 108, 167n63, 171n58
George, Lloyd, 34
Gergen, David, 125–26, 172n80
Germany, 7, 10, 24, 25, 37, 66, 67, 72, 104, 148, 154; and Hitler, 7, 37 (see also Hitler, Adolf; World War II); reunification of, 56, 58, 60t, 61, 128–29 (see also Bush,

Germany (*cont'd*)
George H. W.); and unrestricted
submarine warfare, 23, 32 (*see
also* World War I)
Gladstone, William, 94
Glasnost, 55
Gleason, S. Everett, 167n71
Goldsmith, Jack, 172n89
Gorbachev, Mikhail, 52–57, 62, 65,
70–72, 125–27, 131, 138
Grant, Ulysses S., 27
Great Britain, 3, 8, 21, 24, 30–31,
37–38, 63, 66, 94, 101, 107, 154
Great Depression, 35, 144, 155
Greece, 94
Greenstein, Fred, 49, 120, 124,
171n67, 171n71, 172n77,
172n81, 173n10
Grey, Lord, 33
Guatemala, 121, 122
Gulf War, 56, 71, 128, 130–31
Guthrie, Charles, 170n35
Guyana, 21

Hackman, J. Richard, 161n8
Haiti, 30
Hamby, Alonzo, 69, 165n42,
167n75, 171n67, 171n69
Hampshire, Stuart, 168n9
hard power, 7, 9, 12, 13t, 147
Hardin, Russell, 169n31
Harding, Warren G., 15t, 16, 28
Harriman, Averell, 44
Harrison, Benjamin, 27
Haslam, S. Alexander, 168n5
Heclo, Hugh, 143, 173n10
Hershberg, James, 169n28
Hippocratic oath, 151
Hiroshima, 44, 82
Hitler, Adolf, 7, 34, 36–37, 39–40,
66–68, 72, 78, 86, 87, 113, 114–
16, 161n12
Hoar, George, 103
Hoffmann, Stanley, 170n33
Holsti, Ole R., 48, 165n45
Hoover, Herbert, 15t, 16, 36
Hopkins, Harry, 66
House, Edward M. ("Colonel"), 32
Hull, Cordell, 39

Hungary, 47, 122
Huntington, Samuel P., 135, 173n92
Hussein, Saddam, 128, 130, 140

Ikenberry, G. John, 135, 161n7,
172n92
India, 156
Indonesia, 18
Industrial Revolution, 54, 152
Indyk, Martin, 148, 173n16,
174n24
Iran, 18, 121, 122, 131, 134, 146;
and hostage crisis, 70, 88; and
nuclear proliferation, 144. *See
also* Iran/Contra affair
Iran/Contra affair, 52, 62, 91, 127
Iraq: and George W. Bush, 6, 11, 76,
89, 90, 102, 140–41, 143 (*see
also* Bush, George W.); and Gulf
War, 58, 130–31 (*see also* Gulf
War)
Isaacson, Walter, 44, 165n39,
165n41
isolationism, 3, 16–17, 35, 40, 61,
71
Israel, 44, 57–58, 129, 146

Jackson, Andrew, 94
Jackson, Robert H., 97, 170n43
Japan, 16, 47, 119, 136, 139; and
Pearl Harbor, 39, 66 (*see also*
Pearl Harbor); and Theodore
Roosevelt, 24–25, 63, 101, 103
(*see* Root-Takahira agreement;
Russo-Japanese War;); and Tru-
man, 41, 82 (*see also* Hiroshima;
Nagasaki); in the twenty-first
century, 154, 156, 157, 158
Jervis, Robert, 163n27
Johnson, Chalmers, 172n90
Johnson, Lyndon B., 17, 49, 86,
134, 149
Jolo massacre, 102
just war doctrine, 93

Kagan, Robert, 172n91
Kai-shek, Chiang, 45
Kant, Immanuel, 80, 81
Kellerman, Barbara, 95, 161n12

Kennan, George, 43–47, 68–69, 110, 119

Kennedy, John F., 15t, 134; and Cuban Missile Crisis, 17, 85 (*see also* Cuban Missile Crisis); and Vietnam, 149, 162n24

Kindleberger, Charles P., 172n91

King, Martin Luther, Jr., 150

Kissinger, Henry, 2, 6, 18–19, 26, 50, 105, 111, 161n2, 161n11, 163n5

Knock, Thomas J., 164n18

Knott, Stephen F., 173n9

Knox, Philander, 29

Kohl, Helmut, 56–57, 129

Korean War, 44, 82, 90, 123. *See also* North Korea; South Korea

Kristallnacht, 37

Kuwait, 58

Kuznet, Simon, 4t, 164n24

Lang, Janet M., 162n24

Langer, William, 167n71

Lansing, Robert, 142

Latin America, 36, 122

leader attribution error, 5

leadership theory, 5, 75, 132, 149

League of Nations, 6, 26, 28, 32, 34, 61, 65, 72, 89, 107, 109, 143

Lebanon, 127

Lend-Lease Act, 38, 114

Leninism, 125

liberal hegemony, 5

liberalism, 33, 98

Libya, 147–48

Lieberthal, Kenneth, 148, 173n16, 174n24

Liebman, Lance M., 169n20, 169n23

Lindbergh, Charles, 66–67

Link, Arthur, 109, 171n62

Lodge, Henry Cabot, 34, 65

Logevall, Fredrik, 166n51

Lovett, Robert, 44

Lundestad, Geir, 165n43

Lusitania, 32

MacArthur, Douglas, 44, 72, 82, 117

Machiavelli, 87, 88, 169n26

MacMillan, Margaret, 164n20, 173n7

Madrid Conference, 58

Mahan, Alfred, 22

Malta summit, 56, 130

Manchuria, 34

Mandela, Nelson, 10, 73, 150

Mandelbaum, Michael, 172n91

Manela, Erez, 111, 164n19, 171n60, 171n63

Mann, James, 152, 174n22, 174n29

Marshall Plan, 43, 45, 87, 119, 148. *See also* Marshall, George C.

Marshall, George C., 44–45. *See also* Marshall Plan

Marx, Karl, 2. *See also* Marxism.

Marxism, 2, 125. *See also* Marx, Karl

Matlock, Jack, 53, 166n58

May, Ernest, 22, 42, 163n2

McCarthyism, 47, 69, 121

McCloy, John, 44

McCullough, David, 90, 165n33, 168n11, 171n68

McKinley, William, 22, 43, 63

Mead, Walter, 94, 170n37

Mearsheimer, John, 85, 169n22

Mexican Revolution, 30, 95. *See also* Mexico

Mexico, 3, 31, 32, 95, 107, 108. *See also* Mexican Revolution

Miles, Nelson A., 102

Mill, John Stuart, 80

Missouri, 40, 117

Monroe Doctrine, 3, 21, 106; Roosevelt Corollary to, 24, 101

moral reasoning, 77–78, 80, 85–86, 88, 123, 126

Morgenthau, Hans, 170n36

Moroccan Crisis, 25

Mossadegh, Mohammad, 122

Mukunda, Gautam, 150, 174n26

multipolarity, 19, 50, 72, 138, 155

Munich Agreement, 37

Nagasaki, 81–82

Nasser, Gamal Abdel, 121

National Intelligence Council, 152, 159

National Security Council, 49, 122
Native Americans, 3
North Atlantic Treaty Organization
  (NATO), 41, 43, 56, 87, 90, 147
Nau, Henry, 166n55
Neutrality Act, 38
Newfoundland, 24
Nicaragua, 30, 103, 127
Nitze, Paul, 44, 50
Nixon, Richard, 15t, 18–20, 53,
  120, 138; and opening to China,
  17, 50, 149, 150 (*see also* China);
  influence of Wilson on, 111
Nobel Prize, 23, 101
Nolan, Cathal, 114–15, 169n21,
  171n66
Noonan, Peggy, 51
Noriega, Manuel, 131
North Korea, 42, 44, 48, 57, 78,
  119, 144. *See also* Korean War
North, Oliver, 52
NSC 68, 44
nuclear nonproliferation, 17, 130,
  150
nuclear weapons, 44, 48, 53, 78,
  138; and Eisenhower, 69, 123;
  and Obama, 145–46; and Reagan, 61, 126; and Truman, 82,
  118–19, 123 (*see also* Hiroshima;
  Nagasaki)

O'Hanlon, Michael, 148, 173n16,
  174n24
Obama Doctrine, 147
Obama, Barack, 10, 141, 144–48,
  152–55, 158–59
Olson, Lynne, 165n26
organizational capacity, 12, 13t, 52
Orlando, Vittorio Emanuele, 34, 110

Palestine, 57–58
Panama canal, 30, 101, 103, 106
Pandemics, 154, 156
Pearl Harbor, 39–40, 66, 70, 116,
  139
Peloponnesian War, 154
Pendergast, Tom, 43
Perestroika, 55
persuasion, 9, 48, 84

Philippines, 21–22, 25, 27, 91, 101,
  103, 105–6, 127
Pinker, Stephen, 170n34
Platow, Michael J., 168n5
Poindexter, John, 52
Poland, 34
Potsdam Conference, 41
Powell, Colin, 142
Power, Samantha, 170n39
prisoner's dilemma, 92
Progressive Era, 30
Project Solarium, 46
prudence, 81, 87, 94, 96–98, 99t,
  150–51; and George H. W. Bush,
  58–59, 132t; and Eisenhower, 47,
  49, 122–23, 124t; and Reagan,
  128t; and Franklin D. Roosevelt,
  116t; and Theodore Roosevelt,
  101, 104, 105t; and Taft, 107t;
  and Truman, 118, 120t; and Wilson, 112t
public diplomacy, 33

Quemoy-Matsu crises, 122, 123
Quinlan, Michael, 170n35

Rawls, John, 83, 97, 98, 170n36,
  170n44
Reagan Doctrine, 127
Reagan, Ronald, 15t, 51–55, 57,
  60t, 72, 134, 138, 141; and Gorbachev, 56; as transformational,
  16, 60; assassination attempt on,
  70; inspirational style of, 70, 91;
  organizational skills of, 62; and
  ethical foreign policy leadership,
  125–128, 128t (*see also* Iran/
  Contra affair; Strategic Defense
  Initiative (SDI))
realism, 26, 76t, 76, 98, 109, 115,
  118, 130, 131, 156
Reeves, Richard, 163n28
Rice, Condoleezza, 141, 151,
  166n62, 167n76, 172n85
Riggio, Ronald E., 162n16
Roosevelt, Franklin D., 8, 9, 10, 15t,
  15, 35–40, 43, 60t, 68, 72, 111,
  125, 126, 134, 139, 150, 155;
  background of, 55; and World

War II, 41, 66–67, 87 (see World
War II); and ethical foreign policy leadership, 112–16, 116t; and
post–war order, 42; rhetorical
skills of, 49, 51, 143; transformational objectives of, 11, 60, 137,
149; and Truman, 116, 117; and
USS Greer, 85–86, 124 (see also
USS Greer)
Roosevelt, Theodore, 60, 15t, 16,
21, 22, 23–26, 60t, 63–65, 71,
94, 100; balance of power approach of, 93 (see balance of
power); and ethical foreign policy leadership, 99–105, 105t,
112; and Philippines, 91 (see also
Philippines); and Taft, 26–30,
106; rhetorical skills of, 49;
transformational objectives of,
11, 31, 133, 137; and Wilson,
31–33, 107, 108, 111
Root-Takahira agreement, 25
Root, Elihu, 27, 103
Rosenman, Samuel, 38
Rotberg, Robert, 162n17
Roth, Philip, 66, 167n67
Rothkopf, David, 173n8
Russett, Bruce M., 67, 114, 167n72
Russia, 20, 24, 48, 57, 67, 95, 104,
115, 123, 130, 131, 136, 139,
145, 148, 156. See also Soviet
Union
Russo-Japanese War, 24, 101
Rwanda, 95, 140

Sanger, David, 147, 173n14,
174n23
Sarotte, Mary E., 166n60
Schumpeter, Joseph, 54
Schweizer, Peter, 172
Scowcroft, Brent, 59, 129–30, 141,
172n84, 173n6
Sen, Amartya, 83, 169n18
September 11, 2001, 5, 11, 139, 153
Sestanovich, Stephen, 166n59
Shapiro, Robert, 165n36
Shevardnadze, Eduard, 54
Shultz, George, 52, 151
Siberia, 66

Simonton, Dean K., 162n15
Singapore, 12, 18, 157
Skinner, Kiron K., 166n56
Slaughter, Anne-Marie, 157
smart power, 13t, 147, 155
Smith, Jean Edward, 172n75
Social Darwinism, 22, 101
soft power, 9, 12, 13t, 18, 137, 143,
153, 157, 159; and George H. W.
Bush, 131; and Eisenhower, 48,
120, 121; and Obama, 147, 155;
and Franklin D. Roosevelt, 8;
and Wilson, 33
Somalia, 95, 131
Sorensen, Georgia J., 162n19
South Africa, 73, 127, 156
South Korea, 42, 78, 134. See also
Korean War
Soviet Union, 19, 46, 47, 53–54, 58,
65, 67, 115–16, 121, 136, 138;
collapse of, 16, 50, 55–56, 61,
71; and Reagan, 125–127. See
also Russia
Spain, 21. See also Spanish-
American War
Spanish-American War, 21. See also
Spain
Sputnik, 122
Stalin, Joseph, 43, 54, 68, 72
Stanford prison experiment, 91
Sternberg, Robert J., 162n16
Stevenson, Adlai, 69
Straight, Willard, 64
Strategic Defense Initiative (SDI), 53
Suez Canal Crisis, 122

Taft-Katsura conversation, 25
Taft, William Howard, 15t, 15, 26–
31, 46, 60t, 63–64, 65, 71, 137;
and ethical foreign policy leadership, 106–7, 107t; as incremental, 22–23, 24. See also Taft-
Katsura conversation
Taft, Robert, 46, 69, 72
Tahiti, 88
Taubman, William, 165n38, 167n73
Taylor, Alan J. P., 163n22
terrorism, 79, 127, 140, 144, 154,
156, 158

Thatcher, Margaret, 129
Thomas, Evan, 44, 163n1, 165n39, 165n41
Thucydides, 92, 143
Tiananmen Square, 58, 130
Tilchin, William, 26, 101, 104, 163n4, 171n51, 171n55
Tito, Marshall, 45
Tokyo, 82, 119
Toll, Ian, 167n68
Tonkin Bay resolution, 86
Trachtenberg, Marc, 165n31, 167n70
Treaty of Portsmouth, 24, 104
Treaty of Versailles, 34, 88, 109–10, 111, 129, 149
Truman Doctrine, 43, 148
Truman, Harry S., 9t, 9, 15t, 16, 40–45, 49, 60t, 60, 67–69, 72, 89, 111, 134, 139, 141, 143, 150; and atomic bomb, 81, 82, 102 (see also Hiroshima; Nagasaki; nuclear weapons: and Truman); containment policy of, 46, 129; and ethical foreign policy leadership, 116–20, 120t; and Marshall Plan, 87, 90, 148 (see also Marshall Plan); transformational objectives of, 8, 11, 47, 137, 149
Tucker, Robert W., 18, 163n26
Twain, Mark, 100, 102

Ukraine, 130
unemployment, 18
unipolarity, 15t, 16, 19, 51, 59, 138, 140, 156, 159
United Nations, 9, 26, 48, 69, 89, 95, 115, 119; and the Gulf War, 130–31; Security Council of, 42; peacekeeping operations of, 139 (see also Bosnia; Rwanda)
United States Congress, 11, 25, 29, 32, 95, 109, 127, 128, 130, 142, 143. See also United States Senate
United States Constitution, 11, 51, 73, 104, 115, 118; sixteenth amendment of, 28

United States Senate, 30, 34, 61, 102, 110, 143
United States Supreme Court, 28, 63
USS Greer, 38, 86, 114
Utley, Jonathan G., 165n32

Vandenberg, Arthur, 43, 45
Venezuela, 21, 24
Vietnam, 15t, 17–18, 45, 47–50, 69, 73, 77, 86, 119, 133, 138, 149, 162n24
vision, 7, 12, 13t, 59, 76t, 76, 87, 91, 97, 99t, 143, 151; and George H. W. Bush, 56, 57, 130,132t; and George W. Bush, 142; and Eisenhower, 122, 124t; and Nixon, 20; and Obama, 144–45; and Reagan 51, 70, 128t; and Franklin D. Roosevelt, 8, 115, 116t; and Theodore Roosevelt, 25, 26, 63, 99–100, 101, 104, 105t; and Truman, 44, 90, 117, 118, 120t; and Taft, 106, 107t; and Wilson, 108, 109, 110, 111, 112t, 149

Walker, Samuel, 168n11
Wallace, George, 46
Wallace, Henry, 68–69, 72
Walt, Stephen, 161n1
Walzer, Michael, 79, 168n7, 170n36
Washington, Booker T., 100
Washington, George, 1
Weber, Max, 79–80, 96, 168n8
Weinberger, Caspar, 52
Welch, David A., 162n24
Wiebe, Robert H., 161n4, 163n1, 163n3
Williams, Bernard, 88, 169n27
Wills, Gary, 112, 171n65
Wilson, Woodrow, 7, 9t, 11, 15t, 15–16, 22–23, 28, 31–35, 49, 60t, 64–65, 100, 105, 114, 118, 139; and George W. Bush, 141–43; and commitment of troops to World War I, 39, 42, 71, 93 (see also World War I); emotional intelligence of, 61; and ethical foreign policy leadership, 107–12, 112t;

inspirational style of, 60, 133,
137; and League of Nations, 6,
26, 36, 89; and Mexican Revolution, 95 (*see* Mexican Revolution);
and Versailles Treaty, 34, 88, 149
Winston, Kenneth I., 168n6,
168n14, 168n16, 170n41,
170n45
Winter, David G., 162n15
Wolfers, Arnold, 96, 170n36,
170n42
Wood, Leonard, 102
Woodward, Bob, 173n12
World Bank, 4t
World War I, 4, 23, 31, 35, 37–38,
40, 64, 93, 138, 154

World War II, 16, 19, 35, 41, 45, 46,
67, 72, 81, 109, 116, 128, 133,
149

Yamamoto, Isoroku, 66
Yeltsin, Boris, 131
Yew, Lee Kuan, 12, 157, 162n21
Young, Samuel, 102
Yugoslavia, 45, 58, 131

Zakaria, Fareed, 146, 173n21
Zelikow, Philip, 167n62, 167n76,
172n85
Zimbardo, Philip G., 170n32
Zimmerman, Warren, 102, 171n52,
171n54